D0930369

Gardens of the Gilded Age

A York State Book

GARDENS *of the* GILDED AGE

Nineteenth-Century Gardens and Homegrounds of New York State

M. CHRISTINE KLIM DOELL

SYRACUSE UNIVERSITY PRESS 1986

The author and Syracuse University Press wish to thank the Bowers Foundation for generous support for this book. Their kind assistance with the costs of reproducing the historical photographs has permitted a more complete and visually appealing volume than would otherwise have been possible.

The paper used in this publication meets the minimum requirements of American National Standard for Information Sciences—Permanence of Paper for Printed Library Materials, ANSI Z39.48-1984. ∞

Library of Congress Cataloging-in-Publication Data

Doell, M. Christine Klim.
    Gardens of the gilded age.

    (York State book)
    Includes index.
    1. Gardens—New York (State)—History—19th century.
2. Landscape gardening—New York (State)—History—19th
century.   I. Title.
SB466.U65N73   1986   712'.6'09747   86-1061
ISBN-0-8156-0200-6

Manufactured in the United States of America

To Gerry,
who encouraged me
to take his idea
and run.

M. CHRISTINE KLIM DOELL is a consultant in garden history and landscape preservation planning with projects in New York State, Pennsylvania, and Tennessee. She frequently lectures throughout the northeast on America's landscape and garden heritage. In 1982 with her husband, Gerald Allan Doell, she organized the traveling exhibition, "Gardens of the Gilded Age: New York State Victorian Gardens." The following year, she was awarded an architectural fellowship to expand the research for this book.

Ms. Doell has held faculty positions at both Cornell University and the State University of New York, College of Environmental Science and Forestry, where she has taught a variety of professional courses in landscape architecture. She is an associate member of the upstate New York chapter of the American Society of Landscape Architects.

CONTENTS

PREFACE

LTHOUGH many buildings constructed during the nineteenth century have survived intact, their landscape and garden settings, in most cases, have long since disappeared. Natural cycles of growth and decay, together with changes wrought by man, have left only remnants of the historic landscape: a dilapidated fence post, the arching canopy of a venerable tree, some persistent spring bulbs at a dooryard. Consequently, the meaning of these disparate elements is often obscured, allowing us only to speculate about the garden's original form, function, style, and material.

Our understanding of nineteenth-century gardens and landscapes has also been limited by the documentary sources of the period. Nursery and seed catalogs give a good idea about what plants were used, but tell little about how they were arranged. Consequently, the image they suggest is fragmentary and incomplete. Gardening manuals and periodicals, although more comprehensive, tend to describe and illustrate ideal nineteenth-century gardens and homegrounds, with few of the personal touches which gave each garden a character of its own. Even documented landscape and garden plans can be unreliable, for they were often changed during implementation, or rejected altogether. The photograph, however, "cannot deceive." A correspondent to the *Art Journal* in 1860 observed that, "in nothing can it extenuate; there is no power in this marvelous machine either to add or to take from; we know that what we see must be TRUE," if only for an instant.

Gardens, landscapes and the activities which occurred in them were favorite subjects for photography, itself a relatively new technology by the mid-nineteenth century. From 1850 onward, the most common medium for outdoor photography was the stereoview, two almost identical photographs placed side by side. When seen through a special viewer, the photographs converged, producing a convincing illusion of three dimensions. Photography became even more popular in the 1880s when George Eastman of Rochester, New York, introduced the Kodak, a portable box camera which greatly simplified picture-taking. Consequently, hobbyists and professionals alike could record landscapes and gardens, from the ordinary and commonplace to the extraordinary and unique.

Gardens of the Gilded Age explores the history, design and social function of ornamental gardens and homegrounds in New York State during the latter half of the nineteenth century. Each chapter, which focuses on a different aspect of landscape gardening, is profusely illustrated with historical photographs gathered from museums, libraries, archives, and private collections from all over New York State.

Many of the landscapes and gardens illustrated have disappeared or, if extant, no longer retain their nineteenth-century visual character. Only their photographs remain to reveal their appearance while they were intact, during the period of their popularity. Consequently, *Gardens of the Gilded Age* will be a valuable visual resource not only for historic preservationists, architects, landscape architects, and social historians, but for garden enthusiasts with an interest in history.

The photographs featured in *Gardens of the Gilded Age* were not selected for their aesthetic quality alone, or for their uniqueness. Many show ordinary gardens, which reflect the character of common people in the art and craft of garden making. In some cases, gardens were photographed over and over, enabling us to witness their evolution. More often, however, gardens were captured for only a single moment in time. Taken together, these garden photographs provide a new perspective on American customs in landscape gardening from 1860 to 1917.

I am deeply indebted to many individuals, organizations, and institutions for assistance with *Gardens of the Gilded Age.* In addition to those listed in the picture credits, I gratefully acknowledge the New York State Council on the Arts, and the Educational Facilities Laboratories, a division of the Academy for Educational Development, whose fellowship support made the manuscript possible.

Gardens of the Gilded Age began as a traveling exhibition, organized at The 1890 House in Cortland, New York, and circulated by the Gallery Association of New York State. To all who contributed to the success of the exhibition, I am truly grateful.

For their long-standing confidence in me and this project, my personal thanks go to Janet and Lawrence Bothwell, Professor George Earle, Dr. William Seale, Dr. Roland Wolseley, and especially to my husband, Gerry, who shares my interests and joined me in the research. I would also like to thank our families for their assistance and support in a thousand ways. As this book goes to press, I fondly remember Alma Burner Creek, archivist and garden enthusiast, who gave me my first glimpse of the gardens of the Gilded Age.

Cortland, New York   M. Christine Klim Doell
October 1985

Gardens of the Gilded Age

1

Gardens of the Gilded Age

FEW gardens have been more maligned than those created in America between the Civil War and the First World War. The Gilded Age was, as one critic observed "a period in which taste fell to an ultimate minimum; when iron stags grazed amid concentric circles of pink, blue and white asters; and the shame of Venus was hidden by luxuriant Elephant Ears. In that era, respectable merchants spelled the names of their products across their front lawns with nasturtiums and worked out their Masonic devices in sweet alyssum."[1]

Unfortunately, stereotypes like this have outlived the gardens themselves. Therefore, in order to understand the artistic and cultural significance of the gardens of the Gilded Age fully, we must study them in the context for which they were created. Only then will it be clear that they were much more than a collection of exotic flowers and mass-produced ornament. Gardens and homegrounds created in America between 1860 and 1917 were modern manifestations of nineteenth-century art, science, and industry.

Historians and critics agree that the period which followed the Civil War was one of permanent and accelerating change.[2] The South, emancipated from slavery, was forced to evolve a new kind of economic and social order. The West, no longer a vast frontier of vacant territories, emerged as a new political force, while the East moved relentlessly toward urbanization and industrialization. Change of this magnitude cannot fail to touch the lives of ordinary people in more personal, yet no less significant, ways. In fact, many Americans in the 1870s, '80s and '90s, finding fundamental changes in the way they lived and worked, faced their future with both optimism and anxiety.

Perhaps the most profound changes in nineteenth-century society were those brought about by technology. During this period, mechanized industry largely replaced craftsmanship. Steam-driven machines could assemble products faster and often more cheaply than artisans could by hand. Consequently, objects which were once unknown, or within reach of only a few, became widely available and, therefore, desirable.[3] Techniques of mass manufacture were applied to everything from fancy furniture to farming implements, resulting in an unbelievable proliferation of ready-made goods for house and garden.

Technology, however, was one attribute of nineteenth-century society that had few bounds.[4] Improvements in transportation and communication threatened to break down traditional distinctions between urban and rural living. "But, hark! there is the whistle of the locomotive," wrote Nathaniel Hawthorne in 1844. "It tells a story of busy men, citizens, from the hot street, who have come to spend a day in a country village, men of business; in short of all unquietness; and no wonder that it gives such a startling shriek, since it brings the noisy world into the midst of our slumbrous peace."[5] Before long, Hawthorne's dismay could be echoed nationwide. By 1870, federally subsidized railroads and telegraph lines accomplished what the Civil War had failed to do, by linking city and country, North, South, East, and West, in an uneasy national unity.

Those who benefited most from the network of rails were businessmen and cities, for the locomotive had made possible a national economy based on commerce. Cities and towns along the rapidly expanding routes grew even larger, and new communities flourished where there had been only whistlestops. People and products were on the move, increasing the very tempo of daily living.[6] In the span of a single generation, it seemed, America went from being a loose confederation of farmers, artisans, and merchants, to a nation of businessmen, bankers, bookkeepers, and clerks.

After the Civil War, migration to the city grew from a trickle to a stream. "We cannot all live in cities," lamented the editor of the *New York Tribune* in 1867, "yet nearly all seem determined to do so. . . . With millions of acres awaiting cultivation, hundreds of thousands reject this and rush into the cities."[7] For many Americans, the reasons were obvious. Between 1860 and 1880, the value of manufactures rose nearly three-fold, from $2 billion to $5.5 billion. During the same period, profits from agriculture stayed the same or declined. Since cities were the nerve centers of the new industrial order, they offered superior employment and investment opportunities compared to most rural areas.[8]

"The city is the great center of influence, both good and bad," observed Josiah Strong. "It contains that which is fairest and foulest in our civilization."[9] Fairest were the intellectual and creative opportunities. A higher concentration of taxable properties meant more revenues for cultural amenities. Middle- and upper-class families, their affluence tempered by a moralistic concern for others, demanded better schools and colleges, better churches and better newspapers for all. The city also boasted amenities not generally found in the country: libraries, bookstores, art galleries, scientific and historical museums, theaters, concert halls, and opera houses.[10]

Among the foulest attributes of the city were the increased social problems which seemed to accompany urbanization: crime, chronic illness, insanity, family problems. Moralists argued that the cause was the increasing complexity of the urban environment, and the best cure was exposure to nature, believed to have restorative powers.[11] Many city dwellers perceived that the country was a place of unchanging harmony, where rural life was pursued as it had been in the past, complete with all the moral values Americans found lacking in the present. This belief was no more than a rural myth, for farmers were no more or less wedded to tradition than city dwellers.[12] Nevertheless, the myth persisted.

Public parks were one attempt to bring city dwellers some of the benefits, both real and imagined, of life in the country.[13] Advocates maintained that parks would "humanize the rude, soften and educate and enlighten the ignorant, and give continual enjoyment to the educated . . ."[14] For middle- and upper-class families, suburbs became a popular alternative to city living. They were far enough away from the congestion of the city to share some of the virtues of rural life, but near enough to make daily commuting practical.[15]

It was the garden, however, that was most instrumental in perpetuating traditional values for nineteenth-century Americans. No matter if it consisted only of some potted geraniums on the window sill of a city tenement, the garden represented the longing for America's agrarian past, a tie to the soil that symbolized the beauty or satisfaction directly derived from one's efforts. Perhaps Charles Dudley Warner, editor of the *Hartford Courant,* expressed it best: "To own a bit of ground, to scratch it with a hoe, to plant seeds, and watch the renewal of life—this is the commonest delight, the most satisfactory thing a man can do."[16]

Nature Revealed: The Romantic Revolt

The nineteenth century not only brought about dramatic changes in the way Americans lived and worked, it changed the way they thought about themselves and the world around them. Up until this time, Americans had understood their relationship with the environment strictly through reason and the intellect. Initially, the settlers' mission was to create order out of the wilderness, by clearing forests, making farms, and establishing towns and cities. Once survival was assured, however, Americans began to think more of culture and taste.

During the same period, the dwelling evolved from a log cabin to a stylish residence of wood, brick, or stone favoring one of the formal styles: Georgian, Federal, Roman, or Greek Revival. Symmetry, chaste proportions, and restraint were the order of the day. Likewise, gardens were formal, laid out in geometric patterns, enclosed by a fence, wall or high hedge.[17] House and garden were usually planned together, so they frequently shared a common axis.

During the second quarter of the nineteenth century, however, Americans began to discover a new way to experience the environment: through the senses. Romanticism, which originated in Europe but was taken up with enthusiasm in America, was a radical departure from neoclassical traditions. Formalism was rejected in favor of originality and spontaneity. Imagination and emotion were celebrated over reason and the intellect.[18]

Romanticism was frequently characterized by nostalgia for the preindustrial past, often the medieval or Gothic period in Europe, or a preoccupation with nonindustrial cultures like the Orient. Therefore, scholars interpreted it as a response to the growing complexity of an increasingly industrialized and scientific society.[19] Moreover, romanticism fostered new interest in nature, but the search for understanding was more spiritual and emotional than scientific.

Romanticism profoundly affected all creative endeavors, including literature, music, painting, architecture, and landscape design. American writers were the first to express romanticism by exploring nature as a theme. The poems of William Cullen Bryant, and later works by Emerson and Thoreau, taught Americans to regard nature as a key to self-understanding, not necessarily as a force to be reckoned with. Nature was also used in romantic literature to serve as a foil for society. As they chronicled the changes in rural America, novelists Washington Irving and James Fenimore Cooper made the landscape of upstate New York familiar to readers both home and abroad.[20]

American artists of the nineteenth century sought inspiration from nature as well. Thomas Cole, Asher B. Durand, John Kensett, and Frederic Church depicted the scenic beauty of America with startling reality, but their intentions were moralistic rather than documentary.[21] "The purpose of the landscape," observed modern critic Russell Lynes, "was to remove men from the squalid facts of their lives and to invite them to contemplate the verities, to lose themselves in wonders of forests and plains and mountains, to substitute for the sound of machinery and hooves on cobbles the imagined rush of the waterfall, the song of a bird, the rumble of thunder, the wind in the trees."[22] Cole and his followers, who were nicknamed the "Hudson River School" after one of their favorite subjects, are credited by some for establishing the first truly American tradition in landscape painting.[23]

The romantic revolt in literature and art did not go unnoticed by architects and garden makers. As the fashion for formality declined, irregularity became stylish. Greek Revival temples gradually gave way to Gothic cottages and Italian villas. Architects broke free from symmetrical plans and arranged interiors for convenience, often with verandas, piazzas, bay windows, or balconies. As a result, interior and exterior interpenetrated as never before, and the landscape garden became their medium of exchange.

In the landscape garden imaginary sight lines, rather than geometry, provided the organization. Curving walks replaced those that were straight and direct. Trees and shrubs in natural-looking groups supplanted formal allées, and flower beds, once enclosed near the residence, were scattered at the margins of broad, smooth lawns. It was almost as if nineteenth-century homeowners looked beyond their garden gate to discover a natural order to the landscape which had previously gone unnoticed. From then on, the goal of landscape gardening was to improve the inherent capabilities of the site itself, rather than to impose an artificial order upon it.

Nature Refined: The Romantic Landscape in America

As with romanticism itself, the landscape garden originated in Europe, largely the inspiration of the British. At the beginning of the nineteenth century, however, few Americans had any first-hand experience with it. Nevertheless, several authors addressed the topic quite early in the century. In 1806, Bernard M'Mahon devoted eighteen pages in *The American Gardener's Calendar* to the "modern English style of landscape gardening." By 1828, Thomas Fessenden included a whole chapter on "Landscape and Picturesque Gardens" within his book, *The New American Gardener.* It wasn't until 1841, however, that an American book devoted entirely to the subject of landscape gardening was published. The author was Andrew Jackson Downing (1815–52) of Newburgh, New York.

For many, Downing was the embodiment of the romantic movement in America. He was described as tall, dark, slightly Spanish in appearance, with the manners of an aristocrat. In reality, he was a country boy who grew up along the Hudson River in the shadow of the Catskill Mountains, where the natural beauty of the scenery made an indelible impression. Downing was trained in his brother's nursery as a horticulturist and specialist in fruit culture, but took advantage of every opportunity to study the region's elegant country estates.[24]

Downing was convinced that the physical environment, city or country, affected human behavior for better or worse, but that the opportunity to improve one's own surroundings was within reach of every individual.[25] To that end, he wrote *A Treatise on the Theory and Practice of Landscape Gardening, Adapted to North America.* Although Downing borrowed the concepts directly from British sources, particularly the writings of Humphrey Repton and John Claudius Loudon, the examples he featured were entirely American: Blithewood at Barrytown, Montgomery Place, and Hyde Park, among others. Consequently, many properties in Downing's beloved Hudson River valley were established as the epitome of landscape gardening in America.[26]

According to Downing, two distinct principles could be expressed in landscape gardening: the Beautiful and the Picturesque. The beautiful landscape was characterized by softness and simplicity with quiet streams or placid ponds, sweeping meadows or intimate glades, and majestic trees with foliage that was full and luxuriant. By contrast, the picturesque landscape was woodsy and rustic with varied and irregular features: bold outcroppings of rock, rapid torrents or plunging cascades, and trees with tortured and twisted limbs. Since these principles were derived, in part, from characteristics found in natural scenery, landscape gardeners who imitated nature were said to be designing in the "natural" style.

Downing's success with the *Treatise* encouraged him to continue writing about landscape gardening and architecture. In 1843 he brought out *Cottage Residences,* which affirmed the notion that dwellings and grounds be designed to complement one another. Three years later, he initiated *The Horticulturist: A Journal of Rural Art and Rural Taste,* directed to both practical gardeners and the gentry. This monthly periodical had a dedicated national readership until 1876, when it was discontinued.

Andrew Jackson Downing is significant in the history of American landscape gardening, not for his designs, but for his ability to capture the imaginations of middle-class Americans and inspire them to improve their surroundings.[27] One of his contemporaries put it best when he observed that "the value of Downing's books here has been great, not because of their technical excellence, for they are very poor in that quality, but because they are full of life and interest. It is the man and not the architect that wins the popular ear; and he compels his readers to allow that the subject is entertaining and enjoyable."[28]

While Downing succeeded in bringing nature to the city's edge by popularizing the country or suburban residence, his followers brought nature into the city's heart, by perfecting the naturalistic park in America.[29] Like Downing, Frederick Law Olmsted (1822–1903) and Calvert Vaux (1824–95) believed that the quality of the physical environment affected the well-being of the individual and, in turn, the welfare of the entire community. However, they took Downing's premise one step farther, declaring that a healthful environment was the right of every individual, even if he or she could not afford to retire to the country.[30]

Olmsted and Vaux are perhaps best known for their design for Central Park in 1858. Although not the first public park designed in the natural style in America, Central Park was unprecedented both in scale and in scope.[31] "The view of the landscape is everything," revealed Vaux, "the architecture, nothing." The heart of the original design was to translate "democratic ideas into trees and dirt."[32] With the Greensward Plan, as it was called, Olmsted and Vaux skillfully transformed over eight hundred acres of poorly drained, marginally productive land into scenic parkland for the enjoyment of New York City's nearly 1.5 million inhabitants.

Fortunately, the landscape principles embodied in the design of Central Park were repeated nationwide. Olmsted himself went on to design public parks in the natural style in Boston, Montreal, and Chicago, among others.[33] A growing number of landscape architects and engineers did likewise, in nearly every city in America. For those who frequented the sunny meadows or shady nooks, public parks were more than a respite from the urban environment. They were living textbooks of the principles of landscape gardening, and an example to be followed on a smaller scale at home.

The romantic impulse in landscape gardening had particular appeal for nineteenth-century Americans. Compared to the strict geometry of the neoclassical garden, the romantic landscape allowed real freedom of expression. In this way, it enhanced the inherent diversity found in the natural landscape, from which Americans were deriving their own identity.[34] Moreover, the romantic landscape was democratic. Anyone could try his or her skill at landscape gardening, even if the results fell short of fine art. The danger of romanticism, however, was that individuality might lead to self-indulgence, and creativity to eccentricity. Despite that risk, more nineteenth-century Americans may have come to understand the meaning of romanticism through the landscape garden than through either literature or art, for not everyone wrote or painted, but many expressed their individuality in the design of their own homegrounds. The window box, the flower or vegetable garden, the landscape—all satisfied the need for an environment visually responsive to one's personal efforts. "The pleasures and enjoyment of a garden," wrote a correspondent to *The Horticulturist* in 1850, "by no means depend on its extent, but on its high state of culture and keeping."[35]

New York State: Source of Materials and Methods for Garden-Making

Gardens and grounds in New York State were both representative and prophetic of gardens and grounds in America during the nineteenth century. As early as 1820, New York State was the leader in population, foreign and domestic commerce, transportation, banking, and manufacturing.[36] This premier position in an expanding national economy also distinguished New York State in matters of culture and taste. Examples set by New Yorkers in fashion, decorative arts, and architecture, as well as in gardening, were followed and sometimes improved upon elsewhere. In this manner, what may have started as a fad or fancy in New York often became a national trend with larger, more lasting cultural implications.

Images of New York State's gardens and grounds were carried in the hearts and minds of the pioneers and immigrants who created this nation. Located on one of three major routes west, New York State made the first impression on Yankees and Europeans who traveled through the region during the nineteenth century. Moreover, New Yorkers themselves were on the move. Fully one-quarter of native-born New Yorkers emigrated elsewhere by 1860, taking their garden ideas and experiences with them.[37]

New York State influenced the rest of the nation not only through its example, but also as a leader in the theory and practice of American landscape gardening during the nineteenth century. Distinguished before 1750 as the site of the first commercial nursery in America, New York became the focus of an international horticultural trade by the mid-nineteenth century.

The nursery industry began with the establishment of the Prince Nursery at Flushing, Long Island, in 1737. Like many of the nurserymen who were to follow, William Prince was interested in pomology or fruit growing, believing that a dependable domestic fruit culture would free the Colonies from their reliance upon imported food.

By the beginning of the nineteenth century, however, other plantsmen found the climate and conditions ideal for the culture of fruit and flowers.[38] In 1797, James Blood-good also opened a nursery in Flushing, which carried a small but remarkably varied assortment of ornamental trees and shrubs for its day. Another Flushing nursery, established by Samuel B. Parsons in 1838, became one of the leading horticultural firms of the century by introducing the Japanese discoveries of plant explorer George Rogers Hall (1820–99).

The Long Island nurseries were also the training grounds for nurserymen in other parts of the state. In the late 1830s Patrick Barry, an Irish immigrant, worked as a clerk with the Prince Nursery, learning all phases of the horticulture and nursery business. With George Ellwanger, Barry went on to become a founder of the Mount Hope Botanical and Pomological Garden in Rochester.[39]

In part through the efforts of Ellwanger and Barry, Rochester and the Genesee Valley eventually rivaled Long Island for supremacy in the nursery trade. Although western New York was considered isolated in the eighteenth century, the opening of the Erie Canal in 1825, and the railroads a decade or so later, ushered in a new prosperity during the first half of the nineteenth century. Local inland markets like Rome, Syracuse, and Rochester linked the East Coast with the untapped resources of the West. Direct transport by water from the Great Lakes to the Atlantic cut travel time from Buffalo to New York City from twenty days to only six.[40] These factors, coupled with the advantages of fertile soil and moderate climate,[41] helped western New York take the lead in growing hardy fruits and ornamentals by the mid-nineteenth century.[42]

The Mount Hope Botanical and Pomological Garden, later known as the Ellwanger and Barry Nursery, was by far the largest and most influential nursery in New York State. Begun in 1839 on little more than five acres of land, it grew to become the largest nursery in the world. By 1859, over five hundred acres were devoted to fruit and ornamentals, an area greater than any two other nurseries in America combined. Nearly one hundred acres were planted in ornamentals alone: evergreens, deciduous trees and shrubs, herbaceous and bulbous plants, specimen trees, roses, weeping trees, and the newly-discovered sequoia. This volume was unprecedented at a time when most nurseries were only beginning to grow ornamentals.[43]

After the Civil War, the horticulture industry in New York State expanded to a national market. Ellwanger and Barry established satellite nurseries in Columbus, Ohio, and Toronto, Canada, to serve the demand in Western territories. Sales agents combed Oregon, California, and the Southwest to secure orders of seeds and fruit trees from pioneer homesteaders.[44] Many agents trained by Ellwanger and Barry went on to establish nurseries of their own. Consequently, western New York not only supplied the plants, but also the prototype for the nursery trade to areas beyond the Mississippi River.

Another Rochester entrepreneur launched the seed industry into a national market in the 1870s. James Vick reasoned that areas of the country too remote for nurseries or their sales agents were often accessible by mail.[45] Consequently, he published *Vick's Illustrated Catalog and Floral Guide,* which combined seed listings with practical advice about up-to-date methods for using them. By 1872, mail distribution of the catalog exceeded 225,000 nationwide. Mechanized procedures for seed sorting and packaging enabled Vick to process over three hundred mail orders per day.[46] These improvements revolutionized marketing techniques in the seed industry and set the precedent for seed distribution today.

Horticultural literature published in New York during the Gilded Age was in a favorable position to capture a nationwide audience. As early as 1846, New York State was the center of an active horticultural press. For a comparatively small sum, farmers, homeowners, and hobbyists could subscribe to *The Horticulturist, The American Agriculturist, The Genesee Farmer, The Albany Cultivator,* or *Moore's Rural New Yorker and Country Gentleman.*

These New York State periodicals were recognized as among the best in America, valued for both the number and the quality of subjects addressed. Each month, the editors and a panel of experts reported new developments in horticulture, landscape gardening, rural architecture, botany, pomology, entomology, and rural economy. Letters to the editors revealed that the readership benefited as much from the network of correspondents the periodicals fostered, as from the discussion of practical topics. As a result, New York became the source of the most up-to-date horticultural knowledge available.

Andrew Jackson Downing's *Treatise on the Theory and Practice of Landscape Gardening* (1841) continued to be the standard reference on the subject, revised and enlarged no fewer than nine times before 1900. Other New York writers acknowledged Downing's contributions and ably advanced ideas of their own, but now to more specialized audiences. Anna Warner encouraged women to garden for pleasure or profit. Peter Henderson, author and seedsman, addressed the rural community and the broadest segment of the middle class.[47] Frank J. Scott, Jacob Weidenmann, and Mrs. Schuyler Van Rensselaer directed their advice to upper- and middle-class homeowners in the suburbs.[48]

By the third quarter of the nineteenth century, a stately mansion surrounded by a natural-looking landscape garden particularly appealed to wealthy families who wished to set themselves apart from the growing middle class. New York State had no shortage of sites with great scenic beauty: on Long Island Sound, along the Hudson River, in the Finger Lakes region or the Adirondack or Catskill Mountains. Since many of these areas were not far from cities and towns, affluent businessmen and professionals could find daily or seasonal respite from the often frantic pace of the workplace. Thus, the Gilded Age ushered in a period of large country estates, which prevailed until the early decades of the twentieth century.

The nineteenth-century interest in beautifying homegrounds was not, however, limited to the wealthy. Garden critics were quick to point out that good taste in gardens was more often a question of fitness and appropriateness than of wealth and extent of grounds. As a result, the owners of more modest homes, in city and country alike, were inspired to improve their properties, no matter how small.

In retrospect, the nineteenth century in America marks the period when interest in gardens and gardening spread from the aristocratic owners of large country estates to average Americans. New York State took the lead early in both the theory and the practice of horticulture and landscape gardening. By 1860, garden enthusiasts could grow a bewildering variety of plants for the price of a packet of seeds, and benefit from the latest achievements in horticultural science as reported by the newspapers. One advocate summed up the universal appeal of ornamental gardening in this way: "Gardening art offers this advantage to its lovers: that they can everywhere enjoy it, and that with comparatively small expense they can patronize it on their own account. The poor washerwoman who has hardly time to look at the statue of George Washington in the city park, and scarce enough money to buy a chromo, is quite able to grow geraniums in her window and to have a pretty bed of marigolds and phloxes in the yard."[49]

The Influence of Style and Dilemma of Taste

IN 1899, F. A. Waugh, Professor of Landscape Gardening, observed that "the natural style is unquestionably the favorite in England and America, and probably only less so in France and Germany." He attributed its popularity to a profound bias, perhaps unconscious, for natural scenery: "noble trees, pretty shrubberies, green lawns and cool shadows."[1] Nearly a century had passed since the natural or English style had first been described in American garden literature. Although not always the favorite, the natural style was certainly common in America by the close of the nineteenth century.

When first proposed, the natural style was a radical departure from the traditional American garden. "Our ancestors gave to every part of a garden all the exactness of geometric forms," observed André Parmentier. "They seem to have known of no other way to plant trees, except in straight lines; a system totally ruinous to the beauty of the prospect."[2] Parmentier, a native of France or Belgium who emigrated to New York prior to 1824, is credited with being the first practitioner of the natural style in America.

By mid-century, however, the natural style was advocated for different reasons—namely, its suitability for the climate and conditions of America. According to Patrick Barry, who commented on the present and future of American horticulture in 1853, America seemed preordained to perfect the natural style. "No country in the world is blessed with such natural facilities for attaining, at a very cheap rate, a respectable position in this branch of horticulture. Wherever we turn our face, except on the naked prairie, we see fine natural landscapes, and the material of landscapes. Trees, and shrubs, and plants, scattered everywhere with unsparing bounty: lakes, rivers, quiet streams, rapid torrents, and thundering cascades; mountains and ravines, hills and valleys, blended so beautifully together, as to make our country one stupendous landscape."[3] Indeed, the natural style was expressed so well at Cedarmere (fig. 2.1), the Long Island estate of William Cullen Bryant, that it is difficult to determine just where nature ends and artistry begins.

Despite the strenuous endorsements of the natural style by horticulturists, landscape gardeners and garden writers, the ancient or geometric style persisted in America. During the first quarter of the nineteenth century, people with culture and taste, like John Lincklaen of Cazenovia and William Andrus of Ithaca (fig. 2.2), incorporated formal gardens in the designs of their elegant country estates. Although somewhat reminiscent of traditional American gardens, these differed from their eighteenth-century predecessors by being sited at the side or rear of the residence, rather than prominently in front as before.

By mid-century, other Americans became inspired by the sophisticated formal gardens of Italy and France. These converts to the geometric style delighted in pattern, ornament, and embellishment, rather than naturalistic scenery. Andrew Jackson Downing explained the distinction in this way: "In the English landscape garden one sees and feels everywhere the spirit of nature, only softened and refined by art. In the French or Italian garden one sees and feels only the effect of art, slightly assisted by nature."[4] The organization and detail of the Mackay Estate on Long Island (figs. 2.14–2.16) clearly resemble chateaus and gardens in France. In a more creative way, perhaps, the Bernadini villa on Staten Island (fig. 2.4) and the Ravine at Yates Castle in Syracuse (fig. 2.3) recall the terraced landscapes of Italy. Since these geometric gardens often featured statues, vases, and fountains, they became even more popular with the availability of mass-produced garden ornament.

In choosing between the natural and the geometric styles, homeowners were urged to study the characteristics of the dwelling and its location. Tastemakers ruled that classical villas, like the Patrick Barry residence in Rochester (fig. 2.13), demanded grounds that were elegant and uncluttered, while picturesque cottages required a more irregular treatment. "Just as in the Latin language an adjective must agree with its noun in gender, number and case, so must a garden agree with its environment. It would be as futile to attempt a naturalistic pond in the center of a smooth-shaven lawn as to place a classic Roman nymphaeum in the midst of a wild garden."[5] Despite this sensible advice, however, many homeowners freely combined elements of both garden styles to suit their personal tastes and needs.

The Dilemma of Taste

Through the first half of the nineteenth century, well-developed gardens and grounds offered a good indication of a person's status, since they were relatively rare, and required a great deal of time, money, and effort for effect. As interest in gardens and gardening spread to members of the middle class, the mere presence of an ornamental garden no longer served as a reliable indicator of status. Instead, one's taste and social position were implied through the variety and quality of plants, ornament and architecture in the garden, and the manner in which these elements were displayed. Those wanting to make a good first impression embellished their homegrounds with as much care as they decorated their parlors. If one fancied bric-a-brac, it was sure to appear on the lawn as statues, vases, or fountains. Trees and shrubs dotted the landscape like odd pieces of verdant furniture. Even the parlor carpet had its floral counterpart.

Still it was true that matters of taste were judged by a variable standard, at best, and many insecure homeowners were reluctant to face the dilemma of taste alone. As a result, they sought advice from the experts: a growing number of horticulturists, seed and nurserymen, and landscape gardeners.

Although a few individuals could afford to hire a landscape gardener to advise them on their particular property, nearly everyone could obtain up-to-date information on horticulture and landscape gardening in a wealth of advice literature. From 1841 until the end of the century, Andrew Jackson Downing's *Treatise on Landscape Gardening* and *Cottage Residences* remained standard references on the subjects of landscape gardening and rural architecture. "Nobody, whether he be rich or poor builds a house or lays out a garden without consulting Downing's works; every young couple who sets up housekeeping buys them."[6]

The average homeowner also found an eager ally in seedsmen and nurserymen. Their innovative mail order catalogs lured customers with beautiful color pictures of rare and unusual plants which featured spectacular flowers or exotic foliage. In addition to the newest offerings, many catalogs also contained chatty advice and illustrations on the most modern techniques for displaying plants, as well as a selection of tools and ornaments considered essential for every well-tended garden.

In their efforts to resolve the dilemma of taste, nineteenth-century homeowners were also inspired by the gardens and landscapes they saw around them. Study of natural scenery enabled gardeners to detect and enhance the inherent charms of their own properties, and diminish the flaws. World travel made foreign cultures seem less strange and often intriguing. Stereoviews, engravings, and international expositions frequently accomplished the same objective for those who were less affluent or less ambitious. Consequently, it was not unusual to find exotic plants and garden ornaments from a dozen different countries huddled together on front lawns from New York to San Francisco. Closer to home, many rural cemeteries, public parks, spas, and summer resorts featured elaborately landscaped grounds. Meant to serve as an incentive to strollers, these garden features also became examples to be attempted at home.

If nineteenth-century gardens seem to defy classification, it is because no single style predominated. Although many gardens were designed in the progressive natural style, there were still those that reflected older, more conservative garden traditions. Some homeowners even blended both styles to create unique, if not always tasteful, settings for their homes.

Natural or geometric, large or small, virtually all gardens hinted at the personalities of their creators. The photographs which follow may speak of ethnic background and cultural traditions, personal tastes and needs, hobbies, a fascination with technology and ornament, or a preoccupation with the latest methods in horticulture. Yet despite their inherent variety, all these gardens were characteristically American. Each was attempted with an artistic spirit, fired by the enthusiasm of the period, and influenced, but rarely bound, by the fads and fancies of the gardener's craft.

2.1 William Cullen Bryant at "Cedarmere," c. 1870
Bryant Library Local History Collection, Roslyn, New York

Cedarmere was the Long Island home of poet and journalist William Cullen Bryant from 1843 until his death in 1878. Notations on this photograph indicate that the view, taken in front of the house, "shows the most characteristic and the most beautiful features of Cedarmere." An irregular water feature crossed by a rustic bridge forms the foreground of the view. The west shore, toward Hempstead Bay, is edged with natural-looking plantings of deciduous and evergreen trees. In the distance one can see the hills across Long Island Sound.

The landscape at Cedarmere was composed with such skill that it is difficult to determine just where nature defers to the hand of man. Calvert Vaux, commenting on the appropriateness of the style for a democratic society, suggests that "the great charm in the forms of the natural landscape lies in its well-balanced irregularity. This is also the secret of success in every picturesque village, in every picturesque country house or cottage. Human nature, when allowed a free, healthy scope, loves heartily this well-balanced irregularity, and longs for it in life, in character, and in almost everything."[7]

In essence, Cedarmere manifests Bryant's viewpoint of society in harmony with nature. In 1811, more than thirty years before he made Cedarmere his home, he wrote "Thanatopsis," which contains one of the most eloquent pleas for the pastoral ideal ever written:

> Go forth, under the open sky, and list
> To Nature's teachings, while from all around—
> Earth and her waters, and the depths of air—
> Comes a still voice.[8]

Bryant was convinced that nature could restore an individual's health and well-being. He went on to become one of the earliest and most effective advocates for public parks in America.

2.2 William Andrus Garden and Grounds, Ithaca, New York, c. 1865
Collection of the DeWitt Historical Society of Tompkins County, Ithaca, New York

This mid-century stereoview illustrates how persistent garden traditions could be. In many respects, the Andrus property reflects the formality of American gardens and landscapes during the mid- to late-eighteenth century, rather than 1865. As such, it might more appropriately be called a pleasure ground, for it has few features reminiscent of the naturalistic landscape garden.

Instead of an undulating lawn which resembled a meadow, the Andrus property featured a circular panel of grass, constructed with as much precision as a garden parterre. Marking the center is a fountain or garden vase on a pedestal, probably the most ornamental feature of the grounds. Smaller triangles of turf accent garden paths and join the circle to the rectangular geometry of the whole.

When this springtime photograph was taken, the other garden beds had not yet been planted. Perhaps, according to eighteenth-century traditions, fruits and vegetables were grown, together with ornamental plants. Mature trees and shrubs relate very little to the geometry of the whole, suggesting that they were added incrementally as single specimens.

2.3 The Ravine at Renwick-Yates Castle, Syracuse, New York, c. 1887.
Collection of the Onondaga Historical Association, Syracuse, New York

No visitor to the Renwick-Yates Castle in Syracuse would mistake the ravine for wild nature, although the composition is decidedly in the natural style. The mown lawn, the firm gravel walks and drives confer a careful polish to the scene which speaks not only of order and neatness, but of considerable expense required to maintain the image.

Of the two variations on the natural style which Downing espoused in his *Treatise on Landscape Gardening,* the foreground of this view more closely resembles the "beautiful" mode. The walks and roads flow in easy curves following a natural alignment. The trees, including the evergreens, exhibit a regularity of form and outline; and artistic vases and statuary command attention. However, as the drive passes under the rustic bridge, partially concealed by overgrown vines, the "picturesque" mode becomes more apparent.

Few garden critics advocated combining both variations of the beautiful and the picturesque in a single landscape. Rather, the landscape gardener should choose between simple and flowing forms or striking, irregular, and spirited forms to achieve unity in the composition.

2.4 Bernadini Villa, Staten Island, 1909
Collection of the Staten Island Historical Society, Richmondtown,
Staten Island, New York

It is not surprising to find that New York, with a population so diverse, displayed a similar variety in the design and planting of gardens and homegrounds. Here, immigrants incorporated different ethnic and cultural traditions in their work, yielding results that could hardly be called typical. Garden writers of the nineteenth century attributed this to the fact that "while an Architect was employed to build the house, no professional artist was employed to arrange the grounds."[9] Consequently, the gardens and grounds, perhaps more than the architecture, reflected the time, place, and personality of nineteenth-century homeowners.

In organization and detail, the Bernadini villa on Staten Island could not be farther from the naturalistic ideal of the English landscape style. Except for the lawn, it more closely resembles the classical traditions of southern Europe, where formality and artistic embellishment prevailed. The grape arbors, on either side of the entry drive, have Old World origins, but are used in the overall design in an ornamental way to reinforce sight lines to the residence, which stands silhouetted against the sky. As in Italy, structure and setting are integrated with a terrace. In this case, it is polygonal in shape, and features a tiered fountain at the center and ornamental plantings at the edge. The small trees with the round-headed crowns may be Chinese catalpa (*Catalpa ovata,* formerly *C. bungei*), popularly planted in formal settings because of its regular outline and interesting texture. Just below the terrace is a flower bed in a scroll pattern, like the mosaic or carpet beds created for public parks and gardens in America and abroad from the 1880s onward. All in all, the Bernadini villa represents a unique juxtaposition of old and new, of example and innovation at the turn of the century.

2.5 Dooryard Garden, Unidentified Farmstead, Possibly Schenectady, New York, c. 1880
Collection of Gerald and M. Christine Klim Doell

The tiny dooryard garden pictured here was an obvious source of pride for this rural family and would have conveyed an equally favorable impression upon strangers. "When I see the humblest dwelling, adorned by a yard of shrubbery and flowers, however small, laid out and preserved in order and neatness, I consider it a good mark . . . and I enter it with pleasant anticipations, but when I see another dwelling . . . a mere ostentatious mass of bricks and mortar, surrounded by grounds, however spacious, slovenly kept, and barren of the fruits of gentle cultivation . . . I approach the entrance with distrust."[10]

The industriousness of this family is repaid several times over by the health and vigor of their flowering plants. In the foreground at left are garden phlox (*Phlox paniculata*), an old-fashioned favorite, but the plantings midground appear to be roses and dahlias. Dahlias are tender tubers native to Mexico, which were originally available through the horticultural trade from Europe. Before the Civil War cut off trans-Atlantic commerce, however, New York City seedsman Peter Henderson began to grow dahlias for American gardens, thus assuring a steady supply. Curiously, most plants in this dooryard are grown in wooden boxes or barrel halves, plunged into the lawn. This technique would have kept the rose bushes neatly contained, and bulbs out of the reach of burrowing rodents.

2.6 Residence of Samuel B. Hawley, Yonkers, New York, c. 1885–90
Collection of the Hudson River Museum, Yonkers, New York

Because of their dramatic settings, the Hudson Valley residences were among the most celebrated in America. Few landscape elements interfered with commanding views of the river, and in this case, of the palisades beyond. Both the residence and grounds of the Hawley family are alike in their dignity and modesty, traits not entirely typical of domestic properties in the 1880s and '90s. The foundations of the home are devoid of plantings. Only vine-filled window boxes provide the leafy foreground for views from parlors or porches. All other ornamental planting is reserved for the lawns.

Opposite the porte cochere is a circular floral mound of annual plants, with only two varieties to the bed. This style was advocated as early as the 1870s and continued to be popular through the end of the century. Flanking the flower bed are two wooden tubs with trees. The ivy planted at the base not only slowed the evaporation of moisture, but added a rustic touch to a predominantly formal setting. These portable landscape plantings might have been orange trees, bay or laurel trees, or oleander, set out for the summer months from the small conservatory at left.

2.7 Gate House at "Algonac," Newburgh, New York, c. 1888
Collection of F. D. R. Library, Hyde Park, New York

Since lodges and gate houses were situated on the outskirts of large properties, the architect and landscape gardener could take cues from the natural landscape in their design and planting. In essence, each was a prelude to the more varied and extensive house and grounds of the owner.

The gate house at Algonac, pictured here, was conceived in the bracketed mode, a term which referred to the projecting eaves of the roof supported by ornamental brackets. In *Cottage Residences,* Andrew Jackson Downing recommended this style as a truly American dwelling, easily executed and readily adapted to the climate and landscape of this country.[11]

To heighten its picturesque qualities, in addition to providing shade and privacy, this cottage was clothed with vines at bays and porches. Downing recommended several varieties for adorning gate houses: Virginia creeper (*Parthenocissus quinquefolia,* formerly *Ampelopsis*), the trumpet honeysuckle (*Lonicera sempervirens*) and climbing roses, especially the Boursault, double prairie, and English white.[12]

The lodge or gate house was generally the residence of the gardener, or farmer and his family, employed to monitor the comings and goings of strangers. Algonac's gardener, Mr. Scollau, is pictured at the gate.

2.8 Grounds of a Suburban Rochester Residence, c. 1895
Ellwanger and Barry Collection, Department of Rare Books and Special Collections, The University of Rochester Library, Rochester, New York

Although garden writers preferred landscapes with varied character, striking views, and native stands of trees, most homeowners had to settle for level sites of limited extent. In these situations, the local nurseryman proved to be a valuable ally for providing as much "nature" as possible.

The porch of this suburban residence, built about 1870, is draped with ivy (*Hedera helix*). Potted plants cluster at the foot of the steps and a rustic planter is poised on the lawn at right. Two young elms (*Ulmus americana*), planted quite close to the residence, will eventually grow to towering heights, enframing the residence from the street. The rest of the lawn is dotted with various ornamental trees and shrubs, to which a new variety was probably added each year. These homeowners had most certainly read the most up-to-date manuals on landscape gardening, for their front walk features a slight inviting curve, and the turf is carefully kept from encroaching on the edges.

Alguire-Gott house
Gardener Scollen at gate

2.9 Lawn of George M. Rich, Binghamton, New York, 1891
Collection of the Broome County Historical Society, Binghamton, New York

Typical of middle-class properties of the late nineteenth century is the lawn of George M. Rich of Binghamton. Huddled within the narrow confines of this lawn are several shade trees, a circular fountain, a popular flowering shrub called the PeeGee hydrangea (*Hydrangea paniculata grandiflora*), and numerous flower beds.

Circular flower beds were the easiest shape to construct and this lawn illustrates several different styles. Some feature masses of a single variety, while others have two or three varieties arranged in concentric rings. Inspiration may have come from seed catalogs, or from the public parks, as the combination of annual flowers with tropical foliage plants, caladium or elephant-ears, was common. Obviously a garden enthusiast, the owner has taken great care to combine only circles in his or her design.

2.10 Approach to "Ashcroft," Geneva, New York, c. 1890
Collection of the Geneva Historical Society, Geneva, New York

The horticultural extravagance of the grounds at Ashcroft in the 1890s belies its tasteful beginnings as a cottage residence of the highest order. Built in 1862 for Amon Langdon and his family, Ashcroft is attributed to Calvert Vaux, one of the most respected architects of the mid-nineteenth century and partner of both Andrew Jackson Downing and Frederick Law Olmsted.

Certainly the elegant garden vase placed appropriately at the intersection of the walk and drive would have been a most suitable embellishment for the grounds of Ashcroft during its early days. In fact a facsimile of this very vase appeared in the eighth edition of Downing's *Treatise on Landscape Gardening,* published in 1853.[13] Even the plant within, a century plant (*Agave americana*), was considered by Downing to be well adapted for garden vases and flower pots because it looked architectural and formal.

As the century progressed, however, this simple garden vase was joined by other accents: potted cycas, dracaenas, and palms. Exotic specimens were introduced into the landscape garden to relieve the monotony of flat, open lawns. Subtropical plants, with large leaves and luxuriant growth, had special appeal for nineteenth-century homeowners. Not only were they recent discoveries of worldwide plant explorations, but they also produced startling effects on the lawn. Subtropicals, transported each summer from the conservatory or greenhouse, contrasted boldly with the texture of hardy trees and shrubs, and made massed plantings of colorful annuals pale by comparison. Consequently, during the last decades of the nineteenth century, exaggeration began to replace subtlety and restraint as desirable qualities in planting design.

2.11 Water Garden and Grounds of James and Sarah Arkell Residence, Canajoharie, New York, c. 1885
Historical Collections, Canajoharie Library and Art Gallery, Canajoharie, New York

2.12 Arkell Gardens Looking West, Canajoharie, New York, c. 1885
Historical Collections, Canajoharie Library and Art Gallery, Canajoharie, New York

The James and Sarah Arkell property is both typical and unique. Like many landscapes of the 1880s and '90s in New York State, the lawns of the Arkell residence were embellished with flower beds and punctuated with containers of tropical plants. Rarely, however, is such skill and variety seen in their design and execution.

James Arkell came to America from Oxfordshire, England, in the 1840s. Always an entrepreneur, he tried his hand as an insurance agent, farmer, and newspaper publisher, before he found his greatest success in the manufacture and printing of paper bags. Previously, bags for flour and other commodities were made from cotton grown in the American South. During and after the Civil War, however, cotton was scarce or unavailable. Arkell was able to win the confidence of doubtful consumers and market bags made from manila paper, which revolutionized the industry.

James Arkell and his wife, Sarah Hall Bartlett Arkell, purchased this Montgomery Street home in Canajoharie in 1868. The Second Empire style house was designed by an architect from Utica, New York, a Mr. Cooper. In the 1890s, this structure was renovated, "encased in stone of different colors, somewhat enlarged and new bay windows added . . . following the English manor motif."[14] It still stands today, operated as a private residence for women.

The gardens and grounds were largely the inspiration of Sarah Arkell, a native of Columbia County, New York. "A lover of the beautiful and aesthetic, she herself seemed a flower among her flower beds. She was so constantly on the lawns among the buds and blossoms that those who [knew] her will always see her among them in her grounds."[15] Under the direction of several gardeners, most notably James Hepburn of Scotland, the lawn was transformed "with the choicest specimens of floriculture, ingeniously and artistically arranged."[16] Laura Arkell Isle Platt, one of five Arkell children, recalled that "the peonies and lilacs grew in profusion. . . . There were six acres in the area of the garden which roughly resembled a flatiron in shape. In this garden was a pool where we children learned to skate. There was also a summer house beside the pool and, as Mother's hobby was flowers, she added a collection (of all colors) of waterlilies to beautify the pool. There were gates from all the sides for entrance of people who wished to view the gardens and to rest in the summer house to enjoy the view across the pool and green lawn stretching toward the house."[17]

Despite its natural look, the pool was entirely man-made. In the fall of 1875, part of the west lawn was excavated and lined with lead, in order to hold the overflow water from a fountain. Beside the pool, a rustic thatch-roofed summer house enframed views across the placid surface to the ornamented grounds and residence beyond. The lawn was frequently the scene of parties with "the grounds brightly lighted with lamps and lanterns."[18]

In 1870, author Frank J. Scott commented that "all women are lovers of flowers, but few American ladies are yet educated in that higher garden culture—the art of making pictures with trees, lawn and flowers."[19] Happily, Sarah Arkell was an exception to that dictum. These gardens were not created in a year or two, but over a period of decades. Only through foresight could Mrs. Arkell be assured that when the picture was finished, every detail would be correct.

2.13 Residence of Harriet and Patrick Barry, Rochester, New York, c. 1890
Ellwanger and Barry Collection, Department of Rare Books and Special Collections, The University of Rochester Library, Rochester, New York

Patrick Barry, proprietor of the Mount Hope Botanical Garden and Nurseries in Rochester, was thoroughly familiar with the prevailing architectural and landscape styles when he built this Italian or Tuscan villa during the middle of the nineteenth century. Since the character of the residence was more formal than picturesque, the grounds were laid out accordingly. The design was in keeping with a principle articulated by Andrew Jackson Downing: "There is no error so frequently committed as to suppose that beauty, whether in houses or grounds, depends on variety and expense. Chasteness, good proportions, agreeable and expressive arrangement of simple forms,—these are the elements of the beautiful, which are always captivating to persons of pure and correct taste."[20]

There are few properties which illustrate the virtue of simplicity better than this. As the proprietor of such a large nursery, Barry might have cluttered his lawns and drives with all sorts of specimens. Instead, he showed restraint. The residence is set within a verdant frame of mature trees. Spiry evergreens in masses, which accentuate the vertical tower at right, are informally balanced by singular specimens of beautifully mounding deciduous trees, probably beeches. The dominant feature of the landscape is a large level lawn, which contrasts dramatically with the architecture. The entrance drive approaches on an even curve and is punctuated at regular intervals by potted palm trees. "It will generally be found that the more simple and natural the arrangement, the more lasting will be the pleasure derived from it," wrote Downing.[21] Today, the property is owned by the University of Rochester.

In 1840, Patrick Barry (1816–90), together with George Ellwanger, founded the Mount Hope Botanical and Pomological Garden, which grew to become the largest nursery in the world. Barry was also a noted writer in the field of horticulture. In 1852, he authored *Barry's Fruit Garden,* which became a standard reference on fruit culture for home and commercial production. In addition, he contributed to numerous horticultural periodicals, including the *Genesee Farmer,* and took over the editorial responsibilities of *The Horticulturist* in 1853 after Andrew Jackson Downing's death.

"Harbor Hill," the Country Seat of Clarence Mackay, Roslyn, Long Island, c. 1905
2.14 Main Approach to "Harbor Hill"
2.15 West Front of the House at "Harbor Hill" before Construction
of Formal Garden
2.16 Versailles Garden at Night
Bryant Library Local History Collection, Roslyn, New York

Long Island was a prestigious address for wealthy businessmen desiring the solitude of a spacious country estate, without forfeiting rapid transit to New York City. Clarence H. Mackay, whose father had made millions from the Comstock Lode, made sure that his was one of the finest. With over five hundred acres, Harbor Hill boasted a magnificent location overlooking Hempstead Harbor at Roslyn.

The development of the estate was less a collaboration than a joint effort by several prominent architectural firms. The residence and lodge, modeled after a French chateau, were designed by McKim, Mead and White. Their work on Long Island residences had been widely acclaimed by the time Harbor Hill was commissioned. Warren and Wetmore, also of New York, were responsible for many of the outbuildings, including the stables, dairy, and farm. Guy Lowell of Boston was retained as the landscape architect. By that time, however, the residence had already been sited on top of the hill, and construction was underway. Lowell's contributions were the layout of the approaches and connecting roads, as well as the design and planting of the gardens and grounds.

As these photographs suggest, views of the chateauesque residence dominated the Harbor Hill estate. According to an article which appeared in *Architectural Record* in 1904, "Mr. Lowell has realized that the way to keep the immediate surroundings of a great house simple, is not to make them artificially natural, but to treat them as frankly artificial — as frankly modified to suit the convenience of the inhabitants, their demand for an appropriate framing of the landscape and effective disposition of vegetation."[22] Therefore, the level area before the crest of the hill was marked for formal treatment, with a more natural treatment as the land began to fall away down the slope.

The immediate approach to Harbor Hill was a broad, straight avenue extending out from the front terrace. Constructing it, however, was no small feat. Originally, this was the location of a deep gully, which had to be filled to accommodate the drive. All the maple trees, planted at regular intervals, were installed as mature specimens, twenty-five feet tall, then trimmed into symmetrical shapes. This allée served as an approach as well as a vista to the south.

Another dramatic vista was created to the west, overlooking Wheatleigh Hills. This was the location of the formal garden which, like the residence itself, was loosely modeled on French precedents. The terrace nearest the residence featured an elaborate pattern of clipped evergreens. These were called embroidery parterres, because they resembled the intricate shapes found in fancy needlework. Immediately below the parterre was the splendid "Versailles" fountain, shown at night in an illuminated hydraulic display. Formal plantings of maple trees, as along the entrance drive, served as both boundary and background for the spectacle.

Verdant Frames

Landscape Elements
and Their Artful Arrangement

IN his 1870 book, *The Art of Beautifying Suburban Home Grounds,* author Frank J. Scott used the words "verdant frame" to describe the artful arrangement of landscape elements around the nineteenth-century home. Scott realized that the task of the landscape gardener, like the artist, was to produce beautiful pictures. The lawn became a canvas to be embellished with plants, rocks, and water. Although nature might provide the inspiration and materials, the landscape gardener had to improve the scene with his or her design. In essence, each composition became a living picture — a verdant frame revealing nature in a more civilized form.

The Lawn

The most important feature of the landscape garden was the lawn — not a rough meadow, but a panel of grass mown to a softness like velvet. Lawns not only gave unity and repose to the landscape picture, but dramatized every other garden feature, as the Brooks and Smith residences in Geneva attest (fig. 3.8). Flower beds, trees and shrubs, or the residence itself stood in sharp contrast to the smooth turf, while sunlight and shadow produced constantly changing patterns on its gentle surface. This effect was so desirable that homeowners attempted to maintain as great an expanse of unbroken lawn as possible, even before the mechanical lawnmower became available.

Trees and Shrubs

The chief ornaments of the lawn were trees, shrubs, and vines, obtained from a variety of sources. Friends and neighbors shared cuttings as readily as they exchanged recipes. Native woodlands offered many fine plants for those who were willing to collect their own. And of course seed and nurserymen competed for the attention of the gardening public with the newest varieties discovered by plant explorers the world over. With this wealth of material at their disposal, homeowners of the last century experimented as never before with achieving novel effects in the landscape.

Unlike homeowners today, people in the nineteenth-century did not feel compelled to conceal the foundations of their homes with a fringe of evergreens. Instead, residences like C. F. Wickwire's in Cortland (fig. 3.11) were accented at the corners or entrances with small flowering shrubs or vines, or were left completely devoid of plantings near the house.

Larger trees and shrubs could be used farther from the residence in masses, for both beauty and practicality. With these, landscape gardeners could enframe a strikingly beautiful view, conceal utilitarian features like drying yards, barns, or vegetable gardens, or give homeowners some privacy from their next-door neighbors. Informal groupings, like those at the Trevor mansion in Yonkers (fig. 3.16), also formed a pleasant background for smaller ornamental trees, flower beds, or garden ornament.

The landscape gardener sometimes selected trees and shrubs for their individual beauty. The best specimens had distinctive characteristics: conspicuous flowers, an unusual growth habit, or foliage with an interesting color or texture, like the Japanese maple at Glenview (fig. 3.13). Planted singly on the lawn, or in a small group, specimens became the object of a view, perhaps from a parlor window, pavilion, or garden seat. The changing seasons produced a kaleidoscope of effects, lending constant variation to the scene.

Used without restraint, specimen plantings could easily disrupt the unity of the landscape composition.[1] Many homeowners, intrigued by things new and unusual, used specimens like verdant furniture, adding a new variety to their lawn each year. Unfortunately, they found that it was much easier to overplant a lawn than it was to overfurnish a room, since trees and shrubs eventually outgrew their assigned spaces.

Vines

If a single kind of plant could characterize the nineteenth-century landscape, it would be the vine. Climbing and creeping vines gave the greatest amount of beauty, with the least care, in the greatest number of places. Without them, landscape gardeners and homeowners, like Harriet Barry of Rochester (fig. 3.14), would have found it difficult to create beautiful garden pictures.

Vines were practical as well as beautiful. A correspondent to *The Horticulturist* in 1849 observed that, "Many are compelled to live in houses which someone else built . . . or which have, by ill-luck, an ugly expression. . . . Paint won't hide it, nor cleanliness disguise it, but vines will do both; or what is better, they will, with their lovely graceful shapes give a new character to the whole exterior."[2]

Vines could also solve a multitude of other garden problems. If summerhouses suffered from too sunny a location, vines shaded and protected them. Flowering vines added even more incentive to linger, for the blossoms would perfume the air with fragrance. Some residences seemed to jump from the lawn like a Jack-in-the-box. Vines at the foundation eased the transition, and mercifully concealed any odd angles or awkward projections. In fact, vines were so versatile that even amateur gardeners made few mistakes in their placement.

Flowers

The proper use of flowers, on the other hand, was most often misunderstood. As an investment in beauty, flowers were hard to resist. Horticulturists and gardeners loved them because flowers demonstrated their skill at growing plants; homeowners loved flowers because they were showier than anything else. Unfortunately, their arrangement on the lawn sometimes resembled "bits of lace or bows stuck promiscuously over the body and skirt of a lady's dress."[3]

Although flowers were essential ornaments, they were introduced only sparingly in the landscape. To be tasteful, homeowners placed flower beds where they could easily be seen, but did not demand attention. Usually this was within sight of the residence, or along its principal walks, as at Fountain Elms in Utica (fig. 3.17).

One system featured flowers in an informal way, arranged in natural-looking drifts of color before a background of dense shrubbery. Bulbs and perennial plants were ideally suited for this "mingled" style, because the succession of bloom produced constantly changing pictures all season long.

Another system featured flowers arranged in geometric-shaped beds. Circles, stars, diamonds, and crescents were incised into the lawn as if with giant cookie cutters. Each spring, the beds were filled with annual plants, to bloom continuously until first frost.

Paths and Pleasure Drives

The task of the landscape gardener did not end with the arrangement of trees, shrubs, vines, and flowers. Sometimes the situation demanded a change in the lay of the land to give grace and beauty to the whole. This skill was frequently put to the test in the design of paths and pleasure drives.

Except on small properties, and those designed in the geometric style, landscape gardeners avoided leading straight to the residence. The most pleasant paths curved gently and approached the residence from a charming angle. Landscape gardeners also avoided unnatural alignments. An easy double curve was preferred to a path which zig-zagged unnecessarily, like the contortions of a wounded snake.

In these ways, the landscape gardener of the nineteenth century imitated natural scenery in order to achieve a more subtle organization of the homeground. This new informality, however, could easily be mistaken for formlessness. As with any experiment, some gardens and homegrounds were more successful than others. Too often, homeowners attempted to crowd the features of more ample grounds into a confined space, creating, at best, an incomplete jumble. Nevertheless, those who used restraint in planting trees, shrubs, vines, and flowers, and sensitively sited paths and drives, could indeed create a garden or landscape which resembled a living picture. Their successes and failures in achieving unity, harmony, and variety in an informal way have shaped the principles used today in the design of residential properties.

3.1 Summerhouse at Williams Residence, Utica, New York, c. 1900
Collection of The Oneida Historical Society at Utica, New York

The term *verdant frame* was most commonly used to convey the similarity between the tasks of the landscape gardener and the landscape artist: that each scene, whether planted or painted, was composed for aesthetic appeal. For many, there was no easier way to signify the location of a special view than with garden architecture. Covered seats, arbors, or summerhouses were sometimes sited in distant parts of the grounds to highlight views of the natural landscape. At other times, they comprised a central feature of a garden, so viewers could appreciate the designed landscape from a favored vantage point.

This two-story summerhouse is probably of the latter variety. Built of wood, ornamented with scroll work and lath, and topped with a Gothic-style birdhouse, it was undoubtedly a cool summer refuge, and a gazebo in the truest sense. (According to legend, the term *gazebo* is derived from the French phrase, "Que c'est beau," which means, "Isn't that beautiful!" The phrase was prompted by the exceptional view from a lookout tower. However, an Englishman present took it to mean the name of the tower itself and called the structure a gazebo.)[4]

3.2 River View from the E. P. Prentice Estate, "Mount Hope," c. 1890
Collection of the McKinney Library, Albany Institute of History and Art, Albany, New York

Mount Hope was a Hudson Valley estate which took advantage of the natural landscape to create a verdant frame for architecture and family activity. The residence was sited on a bank, overlooking a ten- or fifteen-acre lawn which descended to the river. Here, planting was done sparingly, and only in natural looking groups, to heighten the contrast between the sunny meadow and the cool, dark woods. The breadth and simplicity of the landscape, as well as the fine open views, were respected and maintained.

The perspective from the swing illustrates the principle of prospect, by which the landscape gardener created or took advantage of an extended view or vista. Although the distant features of the view are not visible in this photograph, they were described in an Albany periodical: "The view is of uncommon beauty and embraces the city on the left, and the Hudson for many miles below, until lost among the blue hills. The distant peaks of the mountains of Vermont and Massachusetts are distinctly visible. The surface of the river is constantly spotted, during the season, with white sails moving up and down its channel, and the scene enlivened by the occasional arrival and departure of steamboats, and of trains on the Boston railroad, which is seen for many miles from this place."[5]

3.3, 3.4, 3.5, 3.6 Grounds of the Samuel Munson Residence, Utica, New York, c. 1885 Collection of The Oneida Historical Society at Utica, New York

The Munson residence, unlike the preceding property, Mount Hope, had an urban setting, and thus lacked distant views of the natural landscape. In this situation, interest was created by variety in planting. Vines and trailing plants were used: on the façade of the residence, over the central garden pavilion, and along the fences to drape and conceal the flatness of the architectural surfaces. Shade trees created constantly changing patterns of light and shadow, which appeared to modulate the level surface of the lawn. Finally, tropical plants in containers, cycas and century plants, provided portable accents to lawns, paths, and porches, if only for the summer months. Ironically, the straight garden walks culminating in a central garden feature, the enclosure by garden walls, and the relatively small scale of the space are reminiscent of an organization as old as America herself, but the detail and materials of this landscape make clear its "modern" intentions.

3.7 Intimate Garden at "Sonnenberg," Canandaigua, New York, c. 1915
Collection of the Ontario County Historical Society, Canandaigua, New York

Sonnenberg, the summer estate of Mary Clark Thompson, featured a series of ten theme gardens, created during the first two decades of the twentieth century. In scale and organization, the Intimate Garden very easily took on the characteristics of an outdoor room. The marble floor was carpeted at the center with a panel of grass; the walls were adorned with curtains of foliage; and the ceiling was suggested by the leafy canopy of a vase-shaped elm. Even the ornamental plantings were done in utter simplicity, restricted to colors of blue and white. Clearly, this was a garden for rest and relaxation. The skillful use of art out-of-doors, however, prevented tranquility from becoming monotony. The focal point for the entire composition was the tiny marble reflecting pool and the three cherubs whose gestures remained frozen in play.

3.8 Lawn and Plantings Adjoining the Brooks and William Smith Residences, Geneva, New York, c. 1885
Collection of the Geneva Historical Society, Geneva, New York

Many suburban homeowners were dismayed when their neighbors failed to live up to high standards of taste in the embellishment of their homegrounds. Consequently, most landscape gardeners screened views of adjacent properties with borders of trees and shrubs. Not so with the Brooks and Smith residences in Geneva, New York. Theirs was a rare example of how cooperation in design and planting could actually improve the appearance of both properties.

The unifying element in this landscape was the lawn. It stretched from one residence to the other without being broken by fences, walks, or drives. Great care was also shown in the selection and placement of ornamental trees. Most had rounded or weeping forms and, together with the lawn, conveyed smoothness, gentle variation, and grace. According to the prevailing aesthetic, all these were characteristics of the "beautiful" mode, one of several classifications of the natural style of landscape gardening advocated by Downing, then reiterated by others including Scott, Weidenmann, and Waugh.

3.9 Old Homestead of C. G. Durfy, Tompkins County, New York, 1883
Collection of the DeWitt Historical Society of Tompkins County, Ithaca, New York

The unkempt appearance of this Greek Revival farmstead belies the thought which must have gone into its design and planting, because crowded into this small dooryard are all the characteristic features of the nineteenth-century landscape garden: the lawn, ornamental plantings, garden architecture, and ornament.

This lawn, despite its ragged length, was a great improvement over the bare dirt dooryards of many rural dwellings. Turf proved to be a durable material which stabilized the soil and kept the front of the house free from either mud or dust, depending on the season. When labor could be spared, perhaps once or twice during the summer, the lawn had to be mown by hand with a scythe. Otherwise, a sheep, goat, or cow could be tethered to graze, well out of the reach of any prized blossoms.

To these rural residents, the lawn was not the sole ornamental feature of their property. Mature evergreen trees near the dwelling were trimmed of their lower branches to enhance the openness of the front grounds. The boardwalk was edged with ornamental plantings, including a flower bed surrounded by a wire enclosure to protect tender seedlings.

Near the end of the walk were two stumps, perhaps from earlier ornamental plantings which fell victim to old age. Instead of being removed, one was hollowed out and filled with dirt, to receive annual plants—petunias, verbenas, or geraniums—which bloomed all summer. Atop the other stump was a board box, a "natural" plant stand, firmly rooted to the ground and ornamented with a horseshoe for good luck. Stump planters were not only popular on properties with rural or rustic character, but also in resort communities in the Adirondacks, Catskills, and the Thousand Islands.

Trellises also played a role in the form and function of this homeground. At the extreme left of the photograph, a simple ladder-like construction was attached to a rear porch, perhaps to screen the kitchen from view, certainly to provide a shady spot for household tasks like shelling peas or husking corn. At the extreme right was a free-standing trellis with several arm-like projections, obviously made at home with found materials. Since it was the object of the view from the front windows, it probably featured a fragrant flowering vine.

3.10 McGraw-Fiske Mansion Overlooking Cayuga Lake, Ithaca, New York, c. 1885
Collection of the DeWitt Historical Society of Tompkins County, Ithaca, New York

From this perspective of the McGraw-Fiske mansion, it is easy to imagine a scene in Europe along the Rhine, instead of the shores of the Finger Lakes in central New York State. As early as mid-century, one critic observed that "landscape gardening in America, combined and working in harmony as it is with our fine scenery, is already beginning to give us results scarcely less beautiful than those produced by its finest efforts abroad. The lovely villa residences of our noble river and lake margins, when well treated—even in a few acres of tasteful foreground—seem so entirely to appropriate the whole adjacent

landscape, and to mingle so sweetly in their outlines with the woods, the valleys, and shores around them, that the effects are often truly enchanting."[6]

The McGraw-Fiske mansion was designed by architect William Miller in the manner of a French chateau, but the grounds clearly reflect the informal organization reminiscent of the natural or English style of landscape gardening. This can be contrasted with the Mackay estate in chapter 2 (figs. 2.14–2.16), where both house and grounds took inspiration from the French. Designers were frequently more concerned with enhancing the inherent qualities of the site itself, the "genius loci" or spirit of the place, rather than adhering strictly to historical or cultural precedent. Consequently, a chateau or villa in America was not necessarily accompanied by a French- or Italian-style garden.

3.11 Chester F. Wickwire Residence, Cortland, New York, c. 1892
Collection of The 1890 House, Cortland, New York
3.12 Jere Wickwire Astride an Oriental Brass Crane, C. F. Wickwire Residence, Cortland, New York, c. 1895
Collection of The 1890 House, Cortland, New York

Although seemingly stark compared with our current fashions, the landscape setting for the C. F. Wickwire mansion would have been considered tasteful and self-assured for this small city in upstate New York during the 1890s. Unlike the custom for country homes, there was little attempt to unify city houses with their grounds for a naturalistic effect. Consequently, the ornamental plantings, which seem to be no match for the power and grandeur of this façade, serve to accentuate the architectonic effect of the chateauesque style. Only vines were used at the foundation: wisteria to drape the veranda, English ivy (*Hedera helix*) to dramatize the projecting tower, and annual vines loosely gracing the front entry. By 1910, they had completely overpowered the architecture, covering virtually the entire façade in a verdant cloak of foliage.

In addition to the potted century plants (*Agave*) at the base of the front steps, visitors were greeted by a pair of large brass cranes from Japan. These graceful creatures, typical of the Oriental art wares first exhibited at the Philadelphia Exposition in 1876, continued to be very popular with Americans through the close of the century. During the winter months, the Wickwires removed these ornaments from the front lawn and placed them in the front hallway, flanking the inglenook.

Other prominent features of the Wickwire landscape were the circular beds of annual plants, placed symmetrically about the walk on the well-trimmed lawn. Since the front lawn lacked a fence or hedge, in favor of the new "open" style of landscaping, the Wickwires took precautions to protect their ornamentals from small animals. Each bed was ringed by short wooden stakes to which poultry netting was attached. Few people considered it peculiar that the wealthiest man in town used chicken wire so conspicuously on his front lawn. After all, Mr. Wickwire was president of Wickwire Brothers Wire Cloth Mills, and poultry netting was one of the company's major products.

Today the C. F. Wickwire residence, known as The 1890 House, is open to the public as a house museum.

3.13 Howard Nichols, Superintendent of "Glenview," standing by Japanese Maple, Yonkers, New York, c. 1890
Collection of The Hudson River Museum, Yonkers, New York

Specimen trees were part of the palette that landscape gardeners worked with to create beautiful landscape pictures. Always striving for the new and unusual, the landscape gardener in this case selected two natives from Japan to ornament Glenview, the Trevor estate on the Hudson River at Yonkers.

Japanese maples (*Acer palmatum*) were introduced to America as early as 1820, but became popular only after the Parson's Nursery in Flushing began importing them from Europe in the 1850s and '60s. The mature Japanese maple, like the one in the foreground of this photograph, commands respect among garden enthusiasts for its feathery foliage, vibrant blood-red color, and graceful form, eventually spreading wider than it is tall.

Contrasting the Japanese maple was an evergreen false-cypress (*Chaemaecyparis*) with an upright habit and dense, dark green foliage. Introduced from Japan in 1861, it proved to be a superb ornamental tree, and more hardy in New York State than its relative from the Pacific Northwest. Used together, the false-cypress and the Japanese maple created a dramatic tension, which appealed to the nineteenth-century homeowner's love of exaggeration. Some of these specimens still ornament "Glenview," although the property is now known as The Hudson River Museum.

3.14 Hall's Honeysuckle at Patrick and Harriet Barry Residence, Rochester, New York, July 1894.
Ellwanger and Barry Collection, Department of Rare Books and Special Collections, The University of Rochester Library, Rochester, New York

If one class of plants could characterize the nineteenth-century landscape garden, it would be climbing and trailing vines. Prized for their beauty and shade-giving qualities, they were used to cover cottages, verandas, walls, trellises, even the stumps of old trees. The best bloomer of all, according to the Mount Hope Nursery catalogue, was the Hall's Japan honeysuckle (*Lonicera halleana*). This strong and vigorous variety boasted fragrant blossoms of pure white, which gradually turned to yellow. Planted near open windows or on a porch, Hall's honeysuckle was said to perfume the air with its fragrance from July through September. Harriet Barry, wife of the nursery proprietor, is photographed here with her honeysuckle in full bloom.

3.15 "Sunnyside," the Home of Washington Irving, Tarrytown, New York, c. 1890
Collection of The Hudson River Museum, Yonkers, New York

Sunnyside was one of the most highly acclaimed and well-known properties in America and abroad, for it was the residence, from 1832 onward, of noted author Washington Irving. Although he achieved fame in 1809 for his satirical *History of New York,* Irving is perhaps best known for his tales "The Legend of Sleepy Hollow" and "Rip Van Winkle." Descriptions of Sunnyside enliven traveler's accounts, while pictorial engravings of it appear in both literary and horticultural periodicals. Andrew Jackson Downing classified the residence as a "cottage ornée," and wholeheartedly approved of "the charming manner in which the wild foot paths, in the neighborhood of this cottage, are conducted among the picturesque dells and banks."[7] For this, Irving himself can take credit.

Washington Irving referred to his picturesque dwelling as a "snuggery," and certainly its diminutive size and mantle of vines contributed to this image. A Chinese wisteria (*Wisteria sinensis*) embowered both the entrance and gable ends of the home. Vines with contrasting foliage enframed the windows and bordered the foundation. Mid-century favorites for this purpose were the Double Prairie and Boursault roses, the Japan honeysuckle (*Lonicera japonica*), and Virginia creeper (*Parthenocissus quinquefolia*) for fine texture; the Dutchman's pipe (*Aristolochia*) and Grape (*Vitis*) for coarse texture.[8] Today, Sunnyside is a museum property, and open to the public.

3.16 Looking South from "Glenview," Residence of John B. Trevor, Yonkers, New York, c. 1890
Collection of The Hudson River Museum, Yonkers, New York

In a very literal sense, the porte cochere at Glenview, now The Hudson River Museum, provided a verdant frame for this tastefully composed view. The flower bed was placed at the center of a small lawn, skirted by the carriage drive. Tall trees and shrubs formed the backdrop, preventing the viewer from looking beyond the floral focal point.

The flower bed itself was extremely well-manicured, and separated from the lawn by a precisely maintained edge. Foliage plants with identical color, texture, and size gave the bed a uniform appearance. The outer rim might have been begonias, with coleus predominating within. The spike in the center served as a lively accent.

The foreground of the view also featured floral embellishment. The centerpiece was a garden vase filled with trailing vinca and scarlet geraniums, flanked by two smaller arrangements of similar composition. All are unified with the foundation planting of ivy.

3.17 Flower Garden at "Fountain Elms," Utica, New York, 1873–74
Proctor Photograph Collection, Munson-Williams-Proctor Institute, Utica, New York

3.18 Southwest View of Proctor Residence, "Fountain Elms," 1873–74
Proctor Photograph Collection, Munson-Williams-Proctor Institute, Utica, New York

The flower garden at Fountain Elms is a superb example of the appropriate placement and use of flowers in the nineteenth-century landscape. While most homeowners in the 1870s were placing circular beds of annual plants in the center of their lawns, the Proctor family created theirs where it could be best appreciated: at the intersection of garden paths opposite a covered garden seat.

In organization and design, the garden is characteristic of ribbon or "ribband" bedding, a popular style advocated by some garden writers in the horticultural press, as well as in the seed catalogs. Concentric rings of annual plants were installed according to their height, with the tallest varieties in the center. Interesting touches to this composition are the mounds of plantain-lily (*Hosta*) which accent the lawn near the flower bed.

This part of the landscape at Fountain Elms is clearly a pleasure ground. Paths are not straight and direct, but designed to invite the viewer to linger or contemplate the beauty of the scene, while sitting or strolling. The Proctor residence is now a house museum, although the grounds have been severely altered.

3.19 Floral Mound at Residence of Hon. J. McKechnie, Canandaigua, New York, c. 1870
Collection of the Ontario County Historical Society, Canandaigua, New York

Not all homeowners seemed content with the simplicity of a circular flower bed cut in the lawn. The McKechnie residence featured a floral mound like those constructed in the public parks and gardens. Raised above the flat surface of the lawn, these displayed the gardener's skill in both design and construction. The pyramid form, in this example, was enhanced by triangles and diamonds outlined in Dusty Miller (*Centaurea cineraria*). The flat shapes seem to alternate between two other types of foliage or flowers. At the edge of the lawn, a third variety was used. This kind also forms the outline of the flat diamond shapes incised into the lawn. Here, Dusty Miller forms the accent at the center.

Through the foreshortened perspective of the camera lens, the size of this creation appears to rival the residence itself. Judging by the scale of identifiable plants, it was probably no taller than three or four feet. Construction, however, was no small feat. After the soil was mounded up, it was secured with panels of chicken wire to keep the steep sides from eroding. Young plants, installed at the interstices, eventually grew to anchor both wire netting and soil with their fibrous roots. To assure vigorous growth in such an exposed location, the plants had to be watered frequently, often as much as several times a day during periods of drought.

Garden writers often criticized homeowners for attempting these artificial-looking creations, but instead of being laughed down, they became more popular than ever. Wrote one rueful observer, "In what we term false or bad taste and are accustomed daily to observe, we first endure, then palliate, then accept."[9]

3.20 Lawn Plantings at Alice Austen Residence, "Clear Comfort," Hylan Boulevard, Rosebank, Staten Island, New York, c. 1900
Photograph by E. Alice Austen, Collection of the Staten Island Historical Society, Richmondtown, Staten Island, New York

Clear Comfort was the Staten Island home of E. Alice Austen, a talented and prolific amateur photographer who recorded her world from the 1880s to the Great Depression of 1929. The residence was originally a Dutch Colonial farmhouse, built about 1700. During the next century, however, the one-hundred-acre farm was subdivided to build fashionable residences. In 1844, the house and one acre of land were purchased by Alice's grandfather, John H. Austen, who was a successful New York dry-goods auctioneer. Shortly thereafter, he renovated the residence to accommodate his larger and more affluent family. The Gothic Revival additions, including the dormers, roof cresting, and scalloped shingles are attributed to James Renwick, a prominent practitioner of the Gothic style and personal friend of John Austen.

The landscape around this picturesque dwelling has been composed as carefully as its architectural embellishments. By far, the most dramatic feature was the view, overlooking the bay of New York and the Narrows. To take full advantage of this panorama, a broad turf terrace was extended from the front of the house. Anchoring the corners were several large elms (*Ulmus americana*), distinctive in their vase-shaped form. These

had been carefully placed to enframe and enhance the view, rather than to obscure it. Vines draped along the porch literally provided the verdant frame to this simple but elegant composition.

In the foreground of the photograph an inviting path leads from the carriage drive to the rear of the residence. As in the best examples of landscape gardening, paths were sited well below the level of the terrace, making them hardly visible from the lawn. Small Camperdown elms (*Ulmus glabra Camperdownii*), distinctive for their weeping and mounded forms, are used here like living sculpture to punctuate the alignment of the curve. Today, Clear Comfort is open to the public as a house museum.

Art Out-of-Doors

The Embellishment of the Grounds

IN creating beautiful garden pictures, landscape gardeners often required more than trees, shrubs, vines, and flowers to convey the sentiment behind their garden styles. Whether the intention was rustic or rich, many homeowners relied on garden ornament and architecture to provide the artistic focal point.

Garden Architecture

Today home improvement often means building a patio or deck. This is not a new idea, but rather the extension of a trend which started a century earlier. Nineteenth-century Americans, with more money and leisure than their colonial ancestors, began to see the potential of their homegrounds for outdoor living.

Like the Albany resident in figure 4.13, families first ventured outdoors by attaching porches, verandas, and balconies to their houses. This successful experiment was sometimes followed by adding terraces, arbors, or pergolas to their gardens, summerhouses and gazebos to their grounds. At best, these embellishments were both beautiful and practical solutions to the problems of climate and comfort. At worst, they were artificial constructions which jeopardized the naturalness of the grounds.

Garden architecture drew the eye, and then the viewer, into the landscape garden. Sometimes the intention was to provide a shady retreat for quiet contemplation, at other times to enhance a strikingly beautiful view. Occasionally, garden architecture provided a different perspective of the surrounding garden or landscape, or simply shaded a well-traveled garden path. Garden architecture could be as simple as a grape arbor behind a modest dwelling, or as elegant as a garden pavilion on a beautiful and prominent knoll. Either possibility vastly increased the potential of many homegrounds for outdoor living.

Plans for garden architecture appeared in most gardening magazines, but copying these clumsy illustrations rarely yielded desirable results. Good design conveyed strength, permanence, and the absence of meaningless ornament. In many communities, local builders or handymen were reliable sources for simple, dignified plans. Otherwise, the homeowner was better off attempting his own design, as long as it was modest and neat.

While most properties did not demand a gazebo or garden house, they did require a wall or fence to keep properties distinct and separate. This essential architecture also offered a degree of protection, for the homeowner of 1870 still had to prevent unattended horses, sometimes with carriages attached, from lunching on the lawn and its flower beds.

While privacy was desirable, shutting off the grounds from all view was considered selfish and undemocratic. The best fences and walls for front grounds were those which were the least seen, and the best seen through. Massive walls of stone or brick were rarely over three feet high. Fences constructed of iron or wire, like those at the Thompson estate in Canandaigua (fig. 4.11), could be taller because they were more transparent. However, even these were painted black, brown, green, or bronze to blend better with the natural landscape.

Garden Ornament

During the first decades of the nineteenth century, garden ornament of lead or stone was too expensive for most Americans to purchase. After 1850, however, new technology and mass manufacture made garden ornament both affordable and desirable, particularly by members of the growing middle class. Landscape gardeners and homeowners alike used garden ornament to accentuate views in the garden and landscape, in much the same way as with garden architecture.

Judging by the frequency with which it occurs in photographs, the garden vase or urn was probably the most popular item for nineteenth-century homegrounds. People loved the classical lines of garden vases, because they contrasted so dramatically with the lawn and landscape. Available in sizes ranging from only ten inches to over four-and-a-half feet, there was a garden vase for almost every pocketbook, and every taste, as the proprietors of the Fancher and Durkee store in Binghamton (fig. 4.10) could probably attest.

Vases came in half-a-dozen basic shapes from Grecian to Gothic, with or without handles or covers, either plain or with decoration. Placed singly at the center of a flower garden, or in pairs along a walk or wall, vases especially enhanced the formal character of grounds near the residence. Furthermore, gardeners were careful to elevate vases on pedestals, so that their elegant proportions could be appreciated at eye level.

Beyond their placement, there was heated debate about the tasteful use of garden vases. Some garden writers adovcated planting them with exotic flowers and foliage. Others decried the practice, complaining that it transformed lovely sculptural accents into mere flowerpots. Most homeowners, like the Alexanders of Staten Island (figs. 4.2 and 4.3), seemed oblivious to the arguments and used garden vases, planted or unplanted, wherever they pleased.

According to prevailing thought, garden vases reflected a taste for the refined beauties of art, yet they were only one manifestation of the classical mode of embellishment. Nineteenth-century homeowners could also bring out the artistic character of their gardens and grounds with classical furniture, fountains, and statuary.

For many Americans, including William P. Williams of Manhattan (fig. 4.18), the classical mode fulfilled a need for order and culture which they found lacking in their own brief history. They looked instead to the glories of past civilizations for ornament and architecture which represented the pinnacle of achievement in the arts. Traditional materials, like marble, terra-cotta, and wood, were shaped, sculpted, formed, and carved to create refined designs of intricate detail, fit both for mansions or more modest grounds. Occasionally, these pieces were real antiquities—scavanged fragments from the ruins of the Ancient World. More often, however, they were modern copies of popular subjects, cast or carved especially for American gardens.

Although its popularity was widespread, the classical mode did not suit everyone, nor was it deemed appropriate for all properties. Compatibility was the test most often applied to garden architecture and ornament. To be judged tasteful, embellishments had to fit in with the general character of the house and grounds. For highly finished villas with formal grounds, the classical mode prevailed. On the other hand, if the house and grounds had natural or picturesque qualities, simple rustic effects were best.

Rustic work was a curious and long-lived fascination inspired directly by natural forms. It was actually an exaggeration of the picturesque: a preference for the untouched, disordered beauties of nature. Consequently, many rustic features resembled the rugged character of the landscape itself.

Originally, rustic work relied on natural elements, so the finished product closely resembled the materials from which it was made. Boulders and stone slabs were assembled to create artificial mounds, grottoes or other features simply referred to as rockwork. Roots, branches, and twigs were used to create garden ornament, architecture, and furniture which was honest and natural, if not always comfortable. Resourceful homeowners, like Moses Ogden of Angelica (fig. 4.17), could make rustic ornament themselves from found materials, while the less talented could purchase rustic pieces from local craftsmen.

The rage for the rustic had little to do with wealth or social position. Many who could afford expensive imported ornament chose, instead, the straightforward approach of the rustic mode. In 1852, Cornelius Tyler Longstreet, a prominent Syracuse businessman, built an immense Gothic residence atop a hill near the city. The grounds, landscaped in the natural style, featured many rustic adornments, including rockwork, a rustic bridge, and an extraordinary gazebo, completely surrounding a living tree (fig. 4.7).

Traditional materials of wood and stone were not the only ones used to convey rustic or classical sentiments. As new materials were perfected, they were put to good use in the American garden. As early as 1850, cast-iron turned ornament-making from an art to an industry.

From the start, the manufacture of cast-iron products was geared to the popular market. Objects and sculptural forms, originally conceived in wood, stone, plaster, or marble, could be cast in iron for mass production. Manufacturers tested the versatility of the new material by making everything from hitching posts, fancy gates, fences and railings, to statues, vases, fountains, and furniture.

Cast-iron also offered real advantages to nineteenth-century homeowners. Rustic work in cast-iron was more durable than its twiggy counterpart, which would quickly deteriorate without a protective layer of tar or paint. In addition, cast-iron allowed manufacturers to introduce new rustic motifs like flowers and vines, which would not have been possible with natural materials.

Garden architecture and garden ornament were clearly modern manifestations of nineteenth-century culture and taste. Garden ornament represented a marriage of art and industry which directly benefited the middle class. For the first time, homeowners like the McCarthys and the Eversons of Syracuse (fig. 4.9) could accomplish a great show of luxury with comparatively little cost. Garden architecture responded to changes in nineteenth-century lifestyle by providing additional incentives for outdoor recreation and leisure. Together, they offered new ways to experience the environment.

4.1 Fountain on Andrus Grounds, Ithaca, New York, c. 1865
Collection of the DeWitt Historical Society of Tompkins County, Ithaca, New York

Garden ornament evolved through several periods during the nineteenth century in America. Classical urns and rustic work were the early favorites, popular from the 1840s onward. The middle decades of the 1860s through the 1880s saw the introduction of sentimental subjects—most notably, children and animals. Late in the century, allegorical and tragic figures became popular, as well as articles imported from abroad.

On the Andrus estate, an early nineteenth-century property designed in the formal style, this stone fountain dominated a large panel of grass near the residence. A young boy supports a bittern on his shoulder, from which a jet of water emanates. The base of the fountain resembles a large boulder sporting naturalistic motifs of mosses and ferns. The effect was not purely classical, nor sentimental, nor rustic, but a conservative combination of all three themes, making it appropriate for a variety of situations.

4.2, 4.3 Grounds of the Alexander Estate, "Effingham," Dongan Hills, Staten Island, October, 1891
Collection of the Staten Island Historical Society, Richmondtown, Staten Island, New York

An immense garden vase was the sole ornament in front of the Alexander residence in 1891. Placed opposite the principal entrance, the singular vase served as the foreground to views of the house and grounds from the elliptical carriage drive. The spading fork and step ladder suggest that the vase had been planted with flowers or foliage until the late October afternoon when these photographs were taken.

Garden vases or urns were universal symbols of gentility during the nineteenth century. Imported vases of carved or composition stone were used at first to give a classic and refined aspect to the situation. By 1855, however, American foundries were ready with copies, available in all sizes. This classical vase, with Rococo Revival handles, was designed to appeal to those with a taste for both the Grecian and the Gothic. Unfortunately, it probably offended purists of either style.

4.4 Rural Cottage Adorned with Trellises, c. 1870
Collection of the Geneva Historical Society, Geneva, New York

Trellises in a multitude of forms graced nineteenth-century homegrounds in city and country alike. This rural cottage boasts no fewer than a dozen different types, many of which were probably hand made.

Trellises could either be placed near the residence, in association with porches and windows, or left free-standing on the lawn. Although the second alternative was commonly seen, particularly on early properties, it was frequently criticized as being unnatural.

In style and material, trellises ranged from rough cedar posts plunged into the ground, to elaborate lyre-shaped constructions featuring the work of a scroll saw. Whether simple or intricate, their purpose was the same: to support the many climbers and vines which nineteenth-century homeowners found so hard to resist.

4.5 Helen Fairchild Seated in Front of "Apple Tree Cottage" at "Lorenzo," Cazenovia, New York, c. 1865
New York State Office of Parks, Recreation and Historic Preservation, Bureau of Historic Sites, Lorenzo State Historic Site, Central Region

This diminutive garden structure was originally a childhood playhouse, constructed about 1850, for Helen Lincklaen Fairchild, who is pictured here as a young woman. Whimsically called "Apple Tree Cottage," it was a landscape garden in miniature. Like many domestic properties of the day, a smooth, well-kept lawn surrounded the playhouse, punctuated only by an oval bed of annual plants. Vines draped the structure, supported by a trellis-like wooden framework attached to the façade. The entrance, near where Mrs. Fairchild is seated, was accented by a free-standing pole or trellis concealed by a tangle of climbing vines.

A popular garden writer cautioned that summerhouses, in particular, "require careful treatment and thoughtful good taste to adapt them quite to the best interests of the whole, natural composition."[1] Apple Tree Cottage, like its garden setting, shared a simple charm, laudable in their day for dignity and restraint.

4.6 View in Garden on the "Heights," Brooklyn, New York, c. 1870
Collection of Herbert Mitchell, New York, New York

This hexagonal gazebo exemplified both good taste and neatness, two requisites for garden houses by the third quarter of the nineteenth century. Its filigreed construction was particularly appropriate on properties with picturesque characteristics, when homeowners needed an effect more refined than rustic, without the formality of classical styles. The lattice work was airy and delicate, constructed with strips of wooden lath fastened to a light frame. Consequently, few examples survive intact today.

As popular as garden houses were during the nineteenth century, they were not unique to the period, or even to America. Their origins in Europe go back as far as the Middle Ages, and even farther in the Orient. Nevertheless, the intent was the same. Whether termed a pavilion, summerhouse, belvedere, gazebo, or teahouse, garden houses served as a sheltered retreat for rest or meditation, specially sited to offer fine views of the surrounding garden or landscape.

4.7 Rustic Retreat at Renwick-Yates Castle, Syracuse, New York, c. 1870
Collection of the Onondaga Historical Association, Syracuse, New York

This rustic pavilion or summerhouse on the Yates property in Syracuse was built around a living tree, very much like those illustrated in Downing's *Cottage Residences* and issues of *The Horticulturist.* The structure is situated on a small knoll, to give the viewer better perspective of the surrounding landscape. Sticks and twigs, applied to the framework like lath, provide partial shade for the comfort of visitors, in addition to supporting climbers and vines.

Rustic work was appropriate near cottages and residences having an informal character, as well as along walks and carriage drives at the farthest part of the grounds. Moreover, the materials for rustic work were readily available on many properties without cost, and designs were limited only by the ingenuity of the homeowner or handyman. The only danger was that, as one gardening authority frowned, "rustic work, like everything else, gets into fashion, and then the whole good taste of the country goes mad about it. All sorts of foolish and ridiculous extravagances are indulged in it."[2]

4.8 Rustic Garden Furniture on the Grounds of the Harter Residence, Utica, New York, c. 1885
Collection of The Oneida Historical Society at Utica, New York

Rustic work was a curious and long-lived style inspired directly by natural forms. Initially, artisans used actual branches and twigs to construct grotesque or fanciful forms. This covered garden settee was typical of what could be created by ordinary homeowners using only found materials. Unfortunately, more than one must have complained of the "rough logs, contorted branches and twisted roots, with all their natural excrescences left on to torture the sitter."[3]

Enterprising industrialists eventually resorted to imitating rustic work for mass-manufacture in cast-iron or cement. Several popular items from an 1872 catalog included a rustic stand with a double vase, and a matching chair and settee for verandas, lawns, and cemeteries.[4]

4.9 Residences and Grounds of Robert McCarthy and Jiles Everson, Syracuse, New York, 1878
Collection of the Erie Canal Museum, Syracuse, New York

As mass-produced garden ornament became more available and affordable, criticism mounted against its indiscriminate use. "To see a lawn filled with statuary, and vases, and miniature temples, and rockwork, and arbors, and gaudy flowers, parading like the ware of a tradesman to catch the eye of the public,—how can one help feeling disgust at such vanity and corrupt taste!"[5]

Nevertheless, the appeal of cast-iron ornament was great among middle-class home-owners, because it gave the impression of luxury and expense at a comparatively low cost. Judging by the variety of objects installed on these Syracuse lawns—reclining stags, garden vases, a classical figure, and a fountain—the McCarthy and Everson families found garden ornament hard to resist. However, they did attempt to achieve a harmonious ensemble by arranging the ornament in pairs along the front walk.

4.10 Garden Vases at Fancher and Durkee Store, Binghamton, New York, c. 1870
Collection of the Broome County Historical Society, Binghamton, New York

In most communities, the general store was a convenient source of garden materials for New Yorkers during the nineteenth century. Along with other domestic articles, these Binghamton proprietors displayed several styles of garden vases, unquestionably the most popular type of garden ornament in the third quarter of the nineteenth century. Fabricated of cast-iron or cast-stone, vases were mass produced and made available to the homeowner at reasonable prices. It is also likely that Fancher and Durkee carried a complete line of tools for garden maintenance, together with a full offering of vegetable and flower seeds. The tradition of marketing seeds in this manner began with the Shakers in eastern New York during the first quarter of the nineteenth century, and continues today in hardware, variety, and grocery stores.

4.11 Southern Gate at "Sonnenberg," Canandaigua, New York, 1913
Collection of the Ontario County Historical Society, Canandaigua, New York

"Tasteful entrance gates are like clothing to a man," advised one garden writer. "When we get to know one well, it makes little difference to us how our friend is dressed. But the dress of a stranger is our first clue to his character. So we get the first impression from the entrance gate and the landscape gardener should give it a close study."[6]

The entrance gate at Sonnenberg shows wrought iron craftsmanship at its best. Each spike and flourish had to be fashioned and applied by hand to achieve the airy, filigreed effect. These techniques cost far more than casting and molding. Therefore, wrought iron set many families apart from the masses, who had to rely on cast-iron gates and fences.

By the beginning of the twentieth century, garden critics translated this economic fact into an indictment against all use of cast-iron in the landscape: "Iron can rarely be introduced into a garden unless it be handsomely wrought into grills for gates or frames for lanterns at an entrance, or used for arches to support roses and other climbers." This critic went on to say that comfortless settees, iron chairs with iron grapevines, iron figures, urns, and fountains were "rubbish for the junk heap, intolerable eyesores to people of taste. Would that they might be banished forever from the American flower garden."[7]

Eventually, the critics got their wish. As garden fads and fancies changed, Venus and her modest garden companions were gradually relegated to less conspicuous positions. Garden vases and urns found themselves gracing cemetery plots instead of pleasure grounds; and iron stags became whimsical ornaments, suitable only for resort retreats and fraternal lodges. The demise of cast-iron was completed during World Wars I and II, when homeowners patriotically contributed their fences, fountains, and figures to renew America's supply of scrap iron for guns and bullets.

4.12 Front Grounds of Unidentified Residence, Possibly in Syracuse or Rochester, New York, c. 1870
Collection of The Oneida Historical Society at Utica, New York

Not all city or suburban properties featured garden arbors, pergolas, and summerhouses, but few lacked front fences. "Fences answer to a want keen and urgent in the ordinary homeowner's heart," reasoned Frank Waugh in *Landscape Gardening,* "that is, to the desire for seclusion and privacy, of the owner's home surroundings."[8] These qualities appear to be more in the mind of the homeowner, because in most cases, fences and walls for front grounds were only about two to three feet tall, hardly an obstacle for the gaze of the curious passerby. Rather than resorting to high hedges or walls, which might brand them as selfish and undemocratic, homeowners maintained propriety with front fences of iron, wire, or wood.

The fence which separates this middle-class city residence from the street is unusual. Ordinarily, fences were constructed with vertical pickets or horizontal rails, which could either be simple or elaborate. The fabrication of this fence, with diagonal members and triangular inserts, is unique — an attempt, perhaps, to combine sturdiness with ornament.

4.13 Woman Seated on Veranda, Albany, New York, c. 1900
Collection of McKinney Library, Albany Institute of History and Art, Albany, New York

Porches and verandas played a special part in the maturing of American domestic architecture. They were an honest adaptation of form and function to the vicissitudes of the American climate. As early as 1842, Downing recognized the veranda, piazza, or colonnade as "a necessary and delightful appendage to a dwelling."[9] They kept the entrance to the residence dry and protected in inclement weather, and frequently became an outdoor living space for family members. They also offered unique opportunities for embellishment.

The severity of this stuccoed residence is disarmed by the gaily striped veranda roof and the ornamental plantings. Although garden critics might not have approved, the effect is of honesty and naiveté, rather than urbane sophistication, a truly personalized landscape. Like many nineteenth-century residences, the veranda or porch is festooned with vines and climbing plants. The climbing rose at the corner was probably most prized for flower and fragrance. Its light color suggests that it might have been the white "Seven Sisters" or "Baltimore Belle," pink "Queen of the Prairie," or the "Yellow Rambler," all popular nineteenth-century climbers.

At the base of each porch support is a miniature flower garden rimmed with rocks, which continues along the edge of the porch. House plants in pots — geranium, Norfolk Island pine, and snake plant — mingle outside with their hardier garden companions. Hanging baskets with trailing plants punctuate the spaces between the columns. Lastly, the window boxes at the second floor provide a colorful accent to the exterior and fragrance to the rooms within. For these reasons, scented plants — geraniums, mignonette, or heliotrope — were frequently used for window gardening.

4.14 Gardeners Tending Grounds of Gould Conservatory at "Lyndhurst," Tarrytown, New York, c. 1885
Collection of Lyndhurst, Tarrytown, New York, a Property of the National Trust for Historic Preservation

Certainly one of the most impressive examples of garden architecture was the conservatory commissioned by Jay Gould for the grounds at Lyndhurst in 1881. Its proportions cannot be fully appreciated in this photograph, for it extended over 376 feet in length, and measured approximately 36 feet wide. In spite of its size, however, the structure has a light, airy appearance accented with Gothic Revival details at the entrance and cupolas. Its framework can still be seen on the grounds of Lyndhurst, a property of the National Trust for Historic Preservation.

The conservatory was described as having one of the finest privately-owned plant collections in the United States.[10] There were separate houses for orchids, palms, camellias, roses, ferns, geraniums, grapes, and peaches, each climate controlled to provide the optimum conditions for plant culture.[11] Depending upon what was being grown, sections of the conservatory were temporarily whitewashed to reduce the amount of light and heat from the sun. In this photograph, the central Palm House, which featured over 320 different varieties, has been whitewashed, together with the entire east wing.

Outside, nine gardeners tend the floral bedding which highlights the conservatory grounds. The arrangement of beds in the lawn is symmetrical about the drive. Within each bed, flowers are limited to one or two varieties of annual plants. The exception is the circular bed before the Gothic doorway, which appears to be a mosaic or pattern bed, planted in cacti and succulents.

The significance of the Gould Conservatory was not only in the size and variety of its collection, but in structural innovations which ultimately affected the design and building of greenhouses in America. Previously, wood had been the favored material for rafters, sills, and gutters. In the Gould Conservatory, Lord and Burnham, horticultural architects and builders, substituted cast-iron, which enabled them to build higher, larger, and lighter than ever before.[12] The local firm went on to build comparable facilities at the New York Botanical Garden in the Bronx, Schenley Park in Pittsburgh, San Francisco's Golden Gate Park, and the Brooklyn Botanic Garden.[13]

4.15 Jardinieres at Alice Austen House, "Clear Comfort," Hylan Boulevard, Rosebank, Staten Island, New York, c. 1900
Photograph by E. Alice Austen, Collection of the Staten Island Historical Society, Richmondtown, Staten Island, New York

Many nineteenth-century gardeners had a mania for collecting. They created arboretums and pinetums to grow the many and varied types of trees; wild and water gardens with particular plant habitats; and rose gardens which specialized in only a single type of plant. But Alice Austen's garden featured a collection of gleaming china and porcelain jardinieres, perhaps acquired by her seafaring uncle, or personally selected during Austen's numerous trips abroad. Interestingly, she uses these opulent-looking artifacts in the landscape as if they were exotic flowers or shrubs.

In this photograph, the narrow walk leading to the rear of the residence is flanked with numerous jars varying in size, shape, and pattern. When possible, similar types have been paired and even planted with the same materials to lend some unity to the scene. To compensate for the irregularity of the ground surface, each piece has been placed on a small level platform; tall ones were even anchored with guylines to prevent them from toppling over. In the minds of some garden critics, this display might have been considered ostentatious, but it probably brought Miss Austen pleasure to know her garden was unique in all the world.

4.16 Unidentified Garden Bower, probably Staten Island, c. 1900–1915
Photograph by E. Alice Austen, Collection of the Staten Island Historical Society, Richmondtown, Staten Island, New York

Contrary to the wishes of most garden writers, rustic trellises, arbors, and garden structures could be found on homegrounds of all types, from picturesque situations where they were favored, to very formal settings. The widespread appeal was due, in part, to their low cost and ease of construction. "Any amateur who can use a saw and hammer can make a rustic arch to grow climbing roses on."[14] After all, when rustic work was completely covered with luxuriant vegetation, it lost its crude look, and could be just as effective in the garden as more expensive materials.

Rustic work could not necessarily be made at the spur of the moment. Boughs had to be cut in the winter, before the sap began to run, then stored to dry and season. If the bark was to remain intact, as in this case, sturdy branches with interesting colors or textures were favored: hickory, red-cedar, cherry, blackthorn, birch, larch, and fir. Otherwise, the bark could be peeled off before construction.

Since this structure was meant to be completely covered with vines and climbers, little care was taken in its fabrication. Four upright posts at the corners supported a framework of poles which were lashed or nailed together for the canopy. As a whimsical touch, a small spherical birdhouse was suspended from the ridge pole.

The garden itself reflects more formal traditions. Focal points are classically styled. The bowl of the recirculating fountain in the foreground features a lion's head and garland motif, atop a simple columned pedestal. A small water jet in the center mists the bog plants within. The circular basin beneath has been planted with waterlilies.

Straight turf paths radiate from the rustic bower in several directions. These are bordered by flower beds before a backdrop of rustic trellises, which create distinct garden rooms, each with its own character. The focal point within the adjacent garden room is a sundial, atop a Gothic pedestal.

4.17 Moses F. Ogden in His Garden, Angelica, New York, c. 1900
Collection of Angelica Free Library, Angelica, New York

The rustic mode is carried to the extreme in the cabin of Moses Ogden of Angelica, a rural community in the southwestern sector of the state. A wagon-maker by trade, Ogden achieved local fame for his collection of natural curios. He is pictured at center right, amid figures and animals fashioned from cedar roots and other found objects. They even ornament the dwelling itself, like rustic gargoyles of some eclectic architecture. This image is significant not only for its unique subject matter, but for the way it illustrates the nineteenth-century compulsion to personalize landscapes. "A garden is no less a garden because it defies all limitations and conventions. And the artistic spirit likewise refuses to be bound by fads and fancies of the gardener's craft. . . . No two gardens, no two human faces, were ever alike. Both have individuality as their chief charm."[15]

4.18 William P. Williams Residence, 4 West 54th Street, West of Fifth Avenue, Manhattan, New York, 1866
U.S. History, Local History, and Genealogy Division, The New York Public Library, Astor, Lenox and Tilden Foundations, New York, New York

This Manhattan brownstone was completed in 1865 for William P. Williams and was later owned by the Rockefeller family. A rectangular space adjacent to the residence was enclosed for the ornamental grounds. The boundary in front was marked by an iron fence, at the rear by a high wall.

The ornamental grounds were planned in the formal style, entirely appropriate considering the rather austere lines of the residence, and the small geometric space allocated. A simple panel of turf was surrounded on three sides with straight walks, except near the street where several evergreen trees were planted. The only other permanent plantings were shade trees, installed at each of the four corners.

One of the most outstanding features of this ornamental ground was the octagonal garden pavilion at the center of the composition. Located directly opposite from the bay window of the residence, it dominated all views, yet from within, would have enframed and isolated scenes, making the grounds seem larger than they were.

In front of the garden pavilion was a large fountain with a circular pool. Water from the simple jet rose perpendicularly, then fell back into a basin, where it dripped to the pool below. So it could be appreciated from every angle, the fountain was surrounded entirely by a narrow walk. Completing the formal setting were six identical garden vases, all planted with flowers. These were placed at equal intervals on the turf, to flank the fountain and garden pavilion.

The site of the William P. Williams residence, together with the undeveloped land to the south, were once part of the Elgin Botanic Garden, developed by Dr. David Hosack (1769–1835). Between 1801 and 1806, greenhouses and hothouses were constructed and nearly twenty acres cultivated for a wide range of plants, including agricultural, native, and exotic species. By 1823, however, the gardens were in ruins, after being abandoned twelve years earlier for lack of funds. During the twentieth century, this site and its surroundings were replaced by Rockefeller Center.

Flower Gardens
Great Effects by Small Means

FEW activities gave the nineteenth-century gardener more satisfaction than the cultivation of flowering plants. Professionals and amateurs alike delighted in the beautiful colors and delicious fragrance which compensated their efforts. Even the most modest households, with comparatively little expense, could grow geraniums in their windows and have a pretty bed of marigolds and phlox in the yard.

Nineteenth-century garden literature makes a greater distinction about the use of flowers in the landscape than we do today. The flower bed was a general term for the place where flowers were installed. In ornamental planting, these were most often associated with walks and lawns. The flower garden, however, consisted of numerous flower beds, all gathered together in one place.

Flower Beds

The ideal situation for a bed of perennial flowers was along a shrub border, garden wall, or woods. There, the irregular growth blended with masses of foliage for a natural effect. Beyond planning for a succession of bloom, the gardener's chief concern was to prevent one plant from obscuring the beauty of another. Therefore, he or she was careful to place small plants in front of taller growing kinds.

Beds of annual flowers earned a prominent position in the nineteenth-century landscape, usually along walks or near the residence. Their dependable and persistent bloom enabled gardeners to mass annuals in patterns. To be effective, each variety of flower or foliage had to be uniform in color, texture, and height. Single plants that died, or grew too large for the arrangement, were removed and replaced. Patches of bare soil were rarely tolerated, even during the hottest or driest summers. When they were done well, however, annual beds evoked the freshness, brilliance, and clarity of precious gems set in the landscape.

Popular systems for bedding out, as it was called, carried delightfully descriptive names. Flower beds at the Albany Orphan Asylum (fig. 5.5) featured ribbon bedding, with row upon row of contrasting flowers. Carpet bedding, a more ambitious style seen in the Formal Garden at Sonnenberg (fig. 5.6), featured elaborate shapes and flat areas of color like the designs in French or Oriental loomed carpets. Each required great technical skill and rare good judgment. Consequently, the strongest argument against the bedding system was the difficulty of finding gardeners who could do it in a truly artistic manner.

Flower Gardens

Scattering flower beds over the lawn was often criticized because the bright splashes of color could interfere with the unity and simplicity of the composition. Landscape gardeners could overcome this fault by concentrating flowers in a single spot: the flower garden.

Flower gardens, like Theodore Irwin's in Oswego (fig. 5.4), could be formal in character, if they were located near the residence. These parterres, as they were called, assisted the transition between the architecture and the landscape. They were sometimes sited on a terrace right next to the dwelling, where they could be enjoyed from a parlor or porch. Other parterres were very private, secluded by a wall or hedge.

Most parterres, like the Grieg garden (fig. 5.1), had geometrical plans: circles, squares, or rectangles crossed by paths of gravel or turf. Beds of flowers were laid out in symmetrical patterns with a sundial, fountain, or vase at the center. A large parterre, like the Lincklaen garden (fig. 5.2), might also feature statues or ornamental trees at the corners or intersections of the paths.

Other kinds of flower gardens were actually specialized parterres. Rose gardens, like the one at Sonnenberg (fig. 5.16), featured bedding roses which bloomed intermittently all summer. For finest effect, the branches were pruned and pegged down, rather than left to grow upright, so that entire beds were covered with foliage and bloom.

Another specialized parterre was the old-fashioned or grandmother's flower garden. These featured annuals and perennials which were old-time favorites: hardy pinks, sweet williams, peonies, sweet peas, and morning glories. In some gardens, even grapes, berries, or fragrant herbs were featured. The plants in old-fashioned gardens were not organized into separate beds for each variety, but were jumbled together to give a casual appearance, reminiscent of some colonial gardens.

Farther from the residence, flower gardens could more closely resemble the character of the grounds. Landscape gardeners could follow lessons learned from nature to enhance the charms or diminish the flaws of each individual property.

Some flower gardens turned difficult spots into real assets. George Ellwanger built a rock garden (fig. 5.11) in an area where stone ledges were natural and could not be removed. It was home to alpine plants—primroses, saxifrages, arabis, campanula, and gentians—which appreciated the cool temperatures and moisture in pockets of soil between the rocks.

Other flower gardens enabled gardeners to feature special collections. Mary Elizabeth Barnes Hiscock planted aquatic and bog plants at the margins of her garden pool for an attractive water garden (figs. 5.9 and 5.10). There, even the wild marsh plants, like sedges, cattails, and sweet-flags mingled charmingly with aristocratic water lilies and Japanese irises.

Wooded areas with winding paths or gently rolling meadows provided an opportunity for wild gardens. The best wild gardens looked like they had not been planned at all. Since regularity completely spoiled the effect, gardeners recommended random planting. Bulbs, like crocuses, squill, snowdrops, and daffodils, were particularly well suited for naturalizing because they could be tossed from the bag by the handful, and planted where they fell.

The widespread popularity of flower gardens in the nineteenth century was not simply because flowers were showy. More than any other landscape element, flowers gave homeowners the opportunity to experiment and truly personalize their homegrounds. For the price of a packet of seeds, gardeners could get great effects. Even if the results were disappointing, they could map out a strategy for improvement the following year.

Flower gardens appealed to both specialists and generalists. There were some who strived to raise perfect plants. Novices could derive as much satisfaction from a massed planting of petunias as the experts did from recreating the optimum environment for a rare and beautiful lily. Others, who valued garden design over the plants themselves, set out to create the most attractive herb garden, perennial border, or rockery. In short, flower gardens offered challenges for gardeners of all abilities and every inclination.

5.1 Garden Parterre of John Grieg, Canandaigua, New York, c. 1865
Collection of the Ontario County Historical Society, Canandaigua, New York

This early nineteenth-century garden in western New York belonged to John Grieg, a wealthy Scotsman, who made another fortune in America as a land agent for Sir William Pulteney. In 1846, Grieg's home in Canandaigua was described by a British visitor as "the finest mansion in town . . . more like a ducal palace than the dwelling of a humble citizen."[1] The sophistication of his garden, although not large, was probably unprecedented for the region.

An outstanding feature of the Grieg garden was the intricacy of its design. Despite the fact that the shape of the overall garden plot was rectangular, there were virtually no flower beds composed solely of right angles. Instead, polygons, arcs, hearts, circles, and paisley shapes were combined to form a pattern which radiated from a six-pointed star. A single garden vase of classical design marked the center. Unlike the gardens of the settlers its owner sought to attract, the Grieg garden reflected the aristocratic traditions of the English Renaissance, transported by wealthy landowners to a new nation.

The Grieg garden was also distinguished for the way plants were arranged: limited to one variety for each bed. In the wisdom of the day, "It is more desirable to be 'profuse of genius' than 'profuse of gold'; a garden of more common plants, displayed in the best possible manner, would excel one full of rarities, unskillfully jumbled together."[2] By 1865, these beds might have contained tea and moss roses, verbenas, dianthus, ageratum, petunia, fuchsia, geraniums, mignonette, or pansies.[3]

5.2 Flower Garden at "Lorenzo," Cazenovia, New York, c. 1865
New York State Office of Parks, Recreation and Historic Preservation, Bureau of Historic Sites, Lorenzo State Historic Site, Central Region

The garden at Lorenzo, the residence of the Ledyard Lincklaen family, is a fine example of a garden in which earlier traditions have persisted. Planned in the first quarter of the nineteenth century, this flower garden retained its geometrical form well into the twentieth century.

The focal point of the garden is a sundial, placed upon a boulder by Ledyard Lincklaen in 1856. Surrounding this is a circular mound of turf, approximately twenty feet in diameter. In this photograph, William Harris, the gardener, rakes the tanbark path marking the central axis of the garden, which extends from the rear of the residence.

The design of the garden is a study in simplicity. Intersecting paths created quadrangular panels of turf, with centers marked by single Norway spruces (*Picea abies*). Choice fruit trees accented the corners. At the edges of each square, bordering the main paths, were narrow flower beds featuring staked specimens of perennial plants.

The Lincklaen garden is much larger than either the tiny dooryard gardens of frontier settlements, or the elaborate, jewel-like parterres of town residences of the same period. Certainly, part of the reason is a suitable site, but more importantly, it reveals the confidence to extend an organization to the larger landscape, possible only when order and culture seemed secure in a region.

5.3 Flower Garden in the Style of a Parterre, Possibly Cortland, New York, c. 1870
Collection of the Madison County Historical Society, Oneida, New York

The natural style of landscape gardening was not suitable for all situations. Even Andrew Jackson Downing, the style's foremost advocate, admitted that where architecture predominated, particularly on small lots, or in close proximity to the residence, the formal, geometric style of gardening still seemed best. At first glance, this central New York garden resembles its colonial ancestors, for the hand of man is overwhelmingly apparent. Closer study, however, reveals a more sophisticated organization based on entirely different premises.

By the 1870s, when this stereoview was taken, gardens no longer needed to be arranged for efficient planting, cultivating, and harvesting. Gardens near the residence were primarily ornamental, planned and planted for their effect as a whole. Consequently, simple squares and rectangles gave way to more elaborate patterns of circles, trapezoids, and other complex shapes. Gone too, was the haphazard arrangement of plants within each bed. Instead, ornamental shrubs or trellised climbers secured the most prominent positions, often with choice bulbous, perennial, or annual flowers planted beneath. Encompassing all was a low edging of ivy, turf, or boxwood, clipped neatly to preserve the outline of the bed and enhance the overall composition of the garden.

Enclosure was still important in the mid-century garden, but primarily for aesthetic and social reasons, rather than for utilitarian ones. Small formal gardens adjacent to residences were often used as open-air salons for viewing or strolling, and privacy from the stares of strangers was essential. At left, a fence with Gothic cresting and open work, which more closely resembles a trellis, screens views of adjacent outbuildings. A dense hedge forms the rear boundary of the garden and a bank or "fall" separates, but does not screen, the residence.

5.4 Flower Garden Behind Theodore Irwin Residence, Oswego, New York, c. 1875
Original Photograph in the Collection of the Oswego Historical Society, Oswego,
** New York**

The tiny parlor gardens which separated many village and farm residences from the street at the beginning of the nineteenth century must have been a delight to passersby, and the pride of residents of the new republic. By the middle of the century, however, the practice fell from favor. Stated one authority, "the flower garden should not be in front of the house. A flower bed judiciously planted and well-kept is, indeed, a delightful spectacle during the short season of its glory, but how short that is! During times of drought or conditions of neglect, sometimes unavoidable . . . the case is very different, and the once smiling parterre becomes often actually repulsive."[4]

The Theodore Irwin residence in Oswego is an excellent example of how outdoor spaces were re-arranged to suit the changing lifestyle ushered in during the nineteenth century in America. New residences were sited much farther from the street than in previous periods, giving homeowners the opportunity to plant a large ornamental lawn in front, where the parlor garden had been. More extensive grounds, together with the ir-

regular architecture of the dwelling, made direct entrance drives obsolete. Often sinuous curves with clustered trees and shrubs replaced formally planted allées. In this 1875 photograph, the service yard with its clothespole is tucked at the rear of the residence, adjacent to the service wing. The flower garden, an ornamental feature, is in full view, opposite the rear porch.

Ironically, this flower garden was the epitome of order and neatness, and would never have put its owner to shame, no matter where it was located. The paths, which required frequent rolling, seem firm and dry. Flower beds are precisely edged with turf, kept clipped. A mixture of annuals, perennials, and roses probably provided a succession of continuous bloom.

These formal parterres were meant to be used, almost like outdoor rooms. During the day, they provided an airy alternative to the darkened interiors of the nineteenth-century residence; in the evening, they afforded a cool respite from the heat of the kitchen or dining room, and an opportunity to walk and talk after a prolonged evening meal.

5.5 Flower Beds at Albany Orphan Asylum, Albany, New York, c. 1880
Collection of the McKinney Library, Albany Institute of History and Art, Albany, New York

Perhaps there is no better gauge of prevailing taste in the nineteenth century than the gardens and grounds of the social institutions of the period. Floral bedding studded the lawns of schools, hospitals, orphanages, and even prisons during the 1870s, '80s and '90s, rivaling those in the public parks. "The beauty of the landscape spoke to the dullest eye, and appealed through it to the most sluggish imagination."[5] This horticultural therapy had the added benefit of training residents in the highly skilled techniques of ornamental planting, in the hope that they might someday market a trade.

Carpet beds, like these at the Albany Orphan Asylum, were not very difficult to construct. Geometric shapes, either simple or elaborate, were cut out of the lawn and filled with masses of annual plants. Usually, the gardener chose one variety to predominate, then accented it with one or more rings of contrasting color. Sometimes several colors of a single variety were used together; otherwise, two or more varieties could be combined. Popular choices for bedding out included coleus, verbena, petunia, geranium, globe amaranth, scarlet sage, and China asters. In this example, the centers of each were accented with a single foliage plant, perhaps yucca or dracaena.

Despite its popularity, floral bedding was not without its critics. Garden writers, who described these fancy flower beds as "pimples on nature's face,"[6] urged homeowners not to recreate these floral monstrosities at home. Others, however, defended the practice, since it indicated the willingness and energy to do something. Nevertheless, advocates and detractors alike had to acknowledge that the floral features were popular, and instead of being laughed down, were more in vogue than ever.

5.6 The Formal Garden at "Sonnenberg," the Estate of Mary Clark Thompson, Canandaigua, New York, c. 1910 *(Bottom, page 93)*
Collection of the Ontario County Historical Society, Canandaigua, New York

Few would deny that great artistic skill would be required in the planning and planting of this floral parterre. However, this was but one of four identical sunken squares which comprised the formal garden at Sonnenberg. Together, they required the annual installation of more than 25,000 plants.

The garden is rectangular in form and extends outwards from the rear of the residence. Gravel paths divide the space into four quadrants. Boxwoods, clipped into pyramids in the French manner, punctuated the vistas across and through the garden. Since these were not hardy in western New York, the boxwoods were planted in tubs, which could be unearthed and moved into sheds for winter storage. Classical ornament and architecture completed the composition, providing the artistic focal points for the formal garden.

Gardens of this size and complexity were hardly typical during the nineteenth century in America. Nevertheless, they suggest the lengths to which garden enthusiasts could go, if they had the wealth, inspiration, and persistence.

5.7 Chinese Peonies in the Lawn, Pictured with George Ellwanger, Rochester Nurseryman, 1899
Ellwanger and Barry Collection, Department of Rare Books and Special Collections, The University of Rochester Library, Rochester, New York

It is difficult to appreciate the scale of this massed planting of peonies, until one discerns the figure of a man in the background. He is George Ellwanger, founder and partner in the Rochester nursery of Ellwanger and Barry. This nursery distinguished itself during the latter half of the nineteenth century as the largest nursery in the world.

Evidently, Ellwanger was fond of the Chinese peony, introduced to America in the early 1800s, and offered no fewer than eighty different named varieties in his catalog. They ranged from the flesh pink "Albert Crousse" and creamy white "Amazone," to the deep purple "Violacea" and delicate rose "Zoe Calot." He described the peony as "a noble flower, almost rivalling the rose in brilliancy of color and perfection of bloom, and the rhododendron in stately growth."[7]

The peony had other attributes which endeared it to the home gardener. It was a dependable plant: hardy, vigorous, and resistant to disease and pests. In addition, no other flower was so well adapted for large, showy bouquets. Ellwanger recommended that it be planted singly on the lawn, in borders, or for a grand show, in a large bed as pictured.

5.8 Charles Frier, Gardener in Informal Garden at "Olana," Hudson, N.Y., c. 1898–1904
New York State Office of Parks, Recreation and Historic Preservation, Bureau of
Historic Sites, Olana State Historic Site, Taconic Region

Olana, a New York State historic site, was originally the residence of landscape artist Frederic Church. In 1890, the informal garden at Olana was progressive indeed. Not a fanciful shape cut into the lawn, nor concentric rings of color, this harmonious garden picture was created from a palette of individual plants arranged to enhance the inherent qualities of each.

By the end of the nineteenth century, homeowners witnessed the demise of the carpet bed, which relied largely upon annual plants, and the emergence of the hardy garden of perennial plants. Wrote one advocate, "Almost every day throughout its long season the hardy garden is changing with the changes of the season. . . . Our garden is never tiresome; its past is a pleasant memory, its future a delightful anticipation, and its bloom an accurate calendar of the seasons."[8]

At first, gardeners had little idea of how to arrange plants in the new informal gardens. Overreacting to the stiff formality of the older style, they resorted to plunging plants here and there with little concern for their effect as a whole. It was only after gardeners imitated how plants naturalized in the wild that their planting schemes became effective compositions.

The informal garden at Olana is skillfully planned and planted, but would never have been mistaken for wild nature. At the right is a wall, clothed in ivy (*Hedera helix*) with Chinese tree peonies (*Paeonia suffruticosa*) at its base. Opposite, the delphiniums are in bloom, backed by herbaceous peonies (*Paeonia officinalis*). Good candidates for the hardy garden were plentiful, including many dependable roses, irises, lilies, phlox, chrysanthemums, astilbe, and ferns.

The most influential exponents of the hardy garden were William Robinson (1838–1935) and Gertrude Jekyll (1843–1932) in England, and Jens Jensen (1860–1951) in America. The thread of continuity which characterizes the work of these three is the firm conviction that the inspiration and design of the garden arises out of its site and conditions. Their corollary, quite naturally, was that native plants were preferable to exotic imports from abroad.

5.9, 5.10 Water Garden, Barnes-Hiscock Residence, James Street, Syracuse, New York, c. 1900
Collection of the Onondaga Historical Association, Syracuse, New York

Hardy plants could be found not only in the flower border, but in the water garden as well. The fragrant white water-lily (*Nymphaea odorata*), native to North America, required a still pool with a trickling inlet and outlet. Dwarf varieties, like those pictured, could even be grown in tubs or half-barrels plunged into the ground. Unlike their tender relatives from the tropics, hardy water-lilies needed no special care once they were established.

The Barnes-Hiscock residence, now the Corinthian Club of Syracuse, featured this series of small pools along a narrow terrace. Each was rimmed with rocks, and embellished with alpine plants and ornamental grasses. Yet, despite the informal way in which the plants themselves were arranged, this composition was far from natural. The alignment of the pools was linear, reinforced by narrow flower borders of perennial plants and dwarf evergreens. To prevent the diminutive scale of this composition from being lost in the larger landscape, views from this garden were screened by a trellised fence. It is likely that this garden terrace was one in a whole series of garden rooms.

5.11 Mr. Ellwanger's Rockery, Rochester, New York, 1894 *(Top, page 101)*
Ellwanger and Barry Collection, Department of Rare Books and Special Collections, The University of Rochester Library, Rochester, New York

Rock gardens, like water gardens, gave homeowners the opportunity to grow an entirely different class of plants than had previously been possible. They became the refuge of unique and interesting alpine plants — the stonecrop, creeping phlox, or hardy candytuft — and others that thrived in the deep, cool, moist pockets of soil not found in conventional gardens. Consequently, care was needed to provide the proper soils, exposure and drainage for plants, so that the rock garden did not degenerate into a rock pile.

Alpine plants were native to the mountainous and glaciated regions of the world. They proliferated at high altitudes where there was little competition from other trees and shrubs. In the wild, they had scarcely enough time to flower before they were buried again by ice and snow. These severe conditions, however, were not requirements for growth. In fact, many thrived in more temperate climates where the summers were longer and rainfall was more moderate. Therefore, these exotic plants did not require the controlled environment of the greenhouse or conservatory to be grown in American gardens.

According to Neltje Blanchan, author of *The American Flower Garden,* most failures to grow alpines and other rock-loving plants resulted from attempting to copy the rockeries of England, instead of adapting them to America's drier, more sunny climate, with extremes of hot and cold.[9] The best rock gardens were either screened from the sun by trees, or situated on northern slopes exposed only to the weaker rays of morning or afternoon sun.

George Ellwanger's rockery was one of the most successful, and worthy of emulation by others. Built on the edge of the lawn at the foot of a wooded slope, it contained many

native and imported flowers and ferns: the tufted phlox or moss pinks (*Phlox sublata, P. procumbens,* and *P. amoena*), the hardy candytufts (*Iberis gibraltica* and *I. corraefolia*), variegated thyme, *Arabis alpina,* hardy alyssums (*Alyssum Wiersbecki* and *A. saxatile compacta*), *Lotus corniculatus,* cowslips and hardy primulas, saxifragas, narcissus, anemones, hepaticas, columbine (*Aquilegia*), helleborus, bloodroot, and violets.[10]

Much of the beauty of this particular garden was the result of its location. The rock ledges occurred naturally in this woodland slope. They were not, like most examples, heaps of stone piled upon a broad, smooth lawn. In addition, the plants were more plentiful than the rocks, an unmistakable sign of successful plant culture. Most important, however, was the skill of the designer. Mr. Ellwanger, mindful of the artistic principles of unity, balance, variety, and rhythm, created a woodland masterpiece which, to the untrained eye, would appear to be genuinely natural.

5.12 Chester F. Wickwire Residence, 17 Tompkins Street, Cortland, New York, c. 1870 Collection of The 1890 House, Cortland, New York

Newcomers to cities and towns were not only immigrants from abroad, but Americans, lured from their homesteads by the promise of prosperity. They brought with them their own traditions, deeply rooted in the rural environment. C. F. Wickwire left the family farm to open a grocery store in Cortland. His home, located only steps away from downtown, contained features which might be considered rural by today's standards. The garden, immediately adjacent to the back door, was cultivated for vegetables and fruit, not for flowers. The rear barn contained the cow, as well as the carriage.

The front grounds were stylish, if simply arranged. Although a pair of young spruce trees flanked the front walk, most of the other ornamental plantings on the front lawn were fruit trees. A wire fence, more affordable than cast-iron and equally ornamental, separated the front lawn from the passersby on the plank sidewalk. Twenty years later, Mr. Wickwire built his new residence on Tompkins Street (see fig. 3.11). By that time, front fences had fallen from favor, and plank sidewalks were replaced by slate, yet the simplicity of the front grounds persisted. There, as here, ornamental features were paired along the front walk.

5.13 Garden Adjacent to House at Southwest Corner of 92nd Street and Central Park West, Manhattan, New York, c. 1873
Collection of the New-York Historical Society, New York, New York

It is hard to imagine that just a century ago, Central Park West (formerly Eighth Avenue) near the reservoir was a dirt road lined with family farms and gardens. Gardens so intensively developed as this were not typical by any means. Separate areas for flowers, vegetables, and fruit were laid out immediately adjacent to a three-story brick residence, from which this photograph was taken. Elsewhere on the site was a narrow framed building with skylights, oriented on a north-south axis, most probably for propagating plants.

Closer study of the flower garden in the foreground of the view reveals a curious blend of old and new. Its organization is nearly identical to a plan for carpet bedding which appeared in Henderson's *Gardening for Pleasure* in the 1870s.[11] Another source from the same period, *Rural Affairs,* recommended symmetrical designs for areas which could be seen "at a birdseye view." They went on to cite an important advantage of this approach: namely, the ease with which additional beds could be made, or the number reduced.[12]

This flower garden differed, however, from carpet bedding. The edging plants appear to be boxwood, maintained at a height of only three to four inches. The area between the beds was shell or stone, instead of turf. The beds themselves were not limited to massed plantings of annuals, but included an assortment of perennial plants. In these ways, the flower garden was reminiscent of the elaborate parterres designed and constructed in England during the eighteenth century and in America until the early nineteenth century. Even the birdhouse, erected on a pole at the center of the garden, recalls earlier traditions, although the vines, trained on strings tied to the top, appear to be a purely Victorian embellishment.

5.14 East Front of L. H. Meyer Residence, "Foxhill," 239 Fingerboard Road, Staten Island, New York, c. 1890
Collection of the Staten Island Historical Society, Richmondtown, Staten Island, New York

Foxhill was the Staten Island estate of Lewis Henry Meyer, a German-born businessman engaged in the shipping, railroad, and banking industries in America. Although his residence was built in 1840, few traces of its original features remain in this photograph. More obvious are the architectural renovations: ornamental brackets, mansard roof, and tower, probably undertaken during the latter decades of the nineteenth century.

Like the residence, the grounds at Foxhill reflected changes in style and taste since the early days. This artificial basin dominated the lawn east of the residence. Planted within were numerous varieties of waterlilies and lotus plants. Until the end of the nineteenth century, this kind of water garden was rarely possible. Most required natural rivulets or streams whose features were "improved" by damming or excavation. With the advent of municipal water systems, however, homeowners could pipe water to their gardens and grounds to create artificial water features.

5.15 Mrs. Haxton and Dog on Piazza, probably Staten Island, New York, October 1893
Collection of the Staten Island Historical Society, Richmondtown, Staten Island,
  New York

During the last quarter of the nineteenth century, garden writers shared little consensus regarding the appropriateness of floral bedding for homegrounds. In *Gardening By Myself,* Anna Warner advocated "ribband beds," similar to Mrs. Haxton's, scattered "here and there" upon a close-shaven lawn.[13] During the same period, *Garden and Forest* was advising their readership that, "exclusive use of coleus, geraniums, alternantheras, echeverias, etc., when arranged in the form of national emblems, mottoes, medallions and other set patterns, cannot be considered elevating in their influence on popular taste."[14]

The choice was critical for the novice, "whose judgment and taste might easily be warped forever by the first book on gardening he may chance to take up." Consequently, the homeowner was urged to consult a variety of sources, "and check off their contradictory statements one against the other, meanwhile using his own eyes out-of-doors, to arrive at a true understanding of what they teach."[15]

5.16 Rose Garden at "Sonnenberg," estate of Mary Clark Thompson, Canandaigua,
  New York, c. 1910 *(Top, page 107)*
Collection of the Ontario County Historical Society, Canandaigua, New York

As garden styles and tastes changed, so did the rose garden at Sonnenberg. From 1863 to 1900, three different rose gardens were laid out, although not necessarily in the same location. This is the third and final incarnation, created at the turn of the century according to the most modern principles of design.

For nearly fifty years, experts had recommended growing roses in masses, with separate beds for each type or color. By the beginning of the twentieth century, this rule of thumb had not changed, although there was considerable difference in the shape of the beds themselves. Sonnenberg's earliest rose garden featured irregularly shaped beds scattered over part of the lawn. By contrast, these beds are formal in outline, symmetrically arranged in arcs about a classically styled pavilion.

Profuse and uniform bloom was not the only criterion for roses at the turn of the century; the garden required contrast and variety as well. Since the price for showy blooms was usually paid by a lack of luxuriant foliage, roses could be difficult to display effectively. Bare dirt or gravel paths made poor settings for the brilliant blossoms, so paths were constructed with turf for contrast.

The other difficulty with rose gardens was their tendency to be flat and monotonous. Fortunately, this problem could be resolved on most homegrounds by using arches, pillars, or trellises for climbing roses. In addition to these devices, Sonnenberg's rose garden featured a two-story iron gazebo, from which this photograph was taken, enabling visitors to get a bird's-eye view of the extensive plantings.

Surrounding the rose garden was a dense hedge of evergreens, installed for practical as well as aesthetic reasons. Not only did they shelter the plants from damaging winter winds, evergreens provided an effective foil for the flowers. More importantly, perhaps,

they preserved an air of mystery about the garden. "To come upon such a garden unexpectedly, through an entrance that gives no hint of what is hidden within, is like suddenly entering Paradise. If a rose garden be forbidding, it is because there is too much design in evidence, and not enough luxuriance of growth to subordinate it."[16]

5.17 Garden at "Rose Hill," Geneva, New York, c. 1889
Collection of the Geneva Historical Society, Geneva, New York

During the first quarter of the nineteenth century, flower gardens required "a commodious piece of good ground, situated in a convenient and well sheltered place, and well exposed to the sun and air."[17] These criteria, set forth by Bernard M'Mahon in *The American Gardeners' Calendar*, aptly describe the garden site at Rose Hill, overlooking Seneca Lake. Located immediately adjacent to the Greek Revival residence, the garden had a southern exposure where it received ample sun all day long.

The garden at Rose Hill was rectangular in shape, divided into smaller blocks for planting. Organized for efficiency, it was a formal garden, informally planted, with plants placed where they would do best. As was customary, the garden was enclosed with a fence or hedge or combination of the two. Despite changes in style and taste, this geometric organization persisted throughout the century. Remnants of what might have been the original boxwood edging still lined the gravel paths in 1889 when this photograph was taken. The planting beds appear to contain a combination of flowers, vegetables, and fruits.

Today, Rose Hill is open to the public as a house museum.

5.18 Perennial Border, Barnes-Hiscock Residence, James Street, Syracuse, New York, c. 1900
Collection of the Onondaga Historical Association, Syracuse, New York

For the most part, America's earliest gardens contained herbaceous perennials, plants whose roots lived year after year in the ground, while the tops died down each winter. These were installed, often rather indiscriminately, in blocks or borders within a set garden. Eventually, however, that style of gardening was rejected by garden makers in favor of small beds of annual flowers scattered about the lawn. It wasn't until the end of the nineteenth century that herbaceous plants were again widely appreciated in American gardens and homegrounds.

In 1909, garden tastemakers considered hardy herbaceous plants and borders to be "an indispensable feature on up-to-date home grounds, although not to the exclusion of the annual fireworks of 'bedding.'"[19] This perennial border, at the Barnes-Hiscock residence, now the Corinthian Club of Syracuse, reflects careful adherence to the most modern principles of garden design at the turn of the century. The border was placed before a background of trees or shrubbery, so that the foliage contrasted well with the color and texture of the blossoms. To enhance the color effects, individual plants were arranged in irregular drifts, numbering six or more. These drifts were often repeated along the border in different combinations, to give unity to the entire composition. Some of the taller plants could occasionally be brought forward so that the masses would not be monotonous. This photograph was taken in June, when the sweet william (foreground) and the Chinese tree peonies (background) were blooming.

Maintaining the Image

Garden Labor

LANDSCAPE gardening was more than simply making plants take root and flourish. One writer called it "the charming art of touching up the truth."[1] Unfortunately, the truth was always ready to assert itself. Before too long, lawns grew ragged, while flowers withered and died. Homeowners were left with the problem of maintaining the image they sought to create.

Wealthy families, like the F. F. Thompsons of Canandaigua, could afford the services of a growing number of landscape professionals to design or simply to tend their city or suburban estates (figs. 6.5 and 6.6). Many of these men had been educated or trained in the great gardens of Europe, but were attracted to this country by rumors of good wages, steady work, and little local competition for employment. America did not have a school of landscape architecture until 1900, so practitioners were either educated abroad or self-taught. A few, like Mr. Adam of Ithaca (fig. 6.1), even learned their trade as apprentices, indentured servants, or slaves. For these reasons, the skills and interests of landscape professionals varied. Homeowners were warned by reputable individuals to be wary of "any ignoramus who styled himself a landscaper." Some mistakes took years to appear and by then, the "landscaper had found employment far away out West, caring very little how his masterpieces in the East may look."[2]

Despite the influx of willing workers, it was advances in science and industry which ultimately revolutionized gardening in the nineteenth century. American ingenuity, applied to the problems of garden maintenance, increased its efficiency and ease. As a result, gardens and grounds could be cared for by individual homeowners (fig. 6.4), without requiring the services of a landscape professional.

One of the first problems of the garden maker was to procure garden plants. Initially, homeowners had to bear the expense of constructing and maintaining their own greenhouse or system of hotbeds, in order to propagate their floral favorites. With the coming of local florists and nurserymen, however, garden makers could rely on extensive commercial greenhouses to meet the increasing demand for new plants for house and garden. The large volume of business transacted by firms like Ellwanger and Barry of Rochester often brought down the cost of plant materials, making them more affordable for Americans of all classes.

The gradual extension of municipal water systems during the nineteenth century gave gardeners what nature had the power to withhold: a reliable source of water. With hoses and sprinklers, gardeners could supplement the traditional sources of the rain-barrel and the pump, thus assuring the very survival of prized plantings during times of drought. City water meant a virtually unlimited supply, plus the pressure enabling it to perform. Therefore, it is not surprising that garden fountains and pools proliferated in the wake of these civic improvements.

By far, the most welcomed development in home gardening during the nineteenth century was the availability of the mechanical lawnmower in 1868. Before its invention, lawns were cut by hand with a scythe. This was a tedious task, done only two or three times a season, and the results varied with the skill of the laborer. Owners of rural properties sometimes got away with grazing their sheep or goats on the grass, but it rarely resembled a velvety carpet.

American ingenuity can only take credit for the practical application of the lawnmower. The inspiration belongs to the British, whose romance with the lawn is even more longstanding than America's. The original mechanism was adapted from machines which trimmed carpet pile, an analogy which now seems fairly obvious. The American version, patented by Chadborn and Coldwell of Newburgh, New York, featured several blades set in a spiral configuration on a cylinder, which could be rolled over the lawn. The implications of the machine were immediate. What had taken four men and a boy more than a week to do by hand could be done by one man with a mower in five or six hours. Convenient, dependable lawnmowers enabled good lawns to become a common sight in America.

Garden Leisure

As new standards of garden maintenance were being set for the lawn, new uses were being found for its broad, smooth surface. By the late nineteenth century, leisure time was no longer considered to be wasteful. Outdoor recreation, which offered fresh air, exercise, and friendly competition, became a favored leisure-time pursuit. The lawn accommodated many activities for growing American families.

Although sports had always been popular with men, croquet was the first game that the whole family could play. No one had an unfair advantage, because it required finesse and skill, rather than strength. The American version was played on the lawn through a course of nine hoops or wickets. The beginning and midpoint of the course was marked with a stake, stump or, as at Rose Hill in Geneva, a planter (fig. 6.9). The object was to strike a wooden ball along the ground with a mallet, through the course and back again, without being sent out of play by the opponent. The croquet craze reached epidemic proportions, affecting a broader public, at one point, than baseball.

Lawn tennis was another game which appealed to both men and women. When it was introduced in 1874, it was meant to provide summer afternoon sport that was not too active for ladies in toe-length dresses. Cortland residents (figs. 6.10 and 6.11) were among those who considered tennis to be healthful and sociable. As its popularity spread among the upper classes, a growing number of women's colleges added tennis to their curricula.

The homeground was a half-way world between the family and nineteenth-century society. There, youngsters could enjoy a rough-and-tumble play on the lawn without scandalizing their elders. Matrons and misses might advance their social status by hostessing lawn parties or luncheons. The homeground became the center of domesticity and leisure in American life, a counterbalance to the world of work.

In middle- and upper-class households, cultivating talent was considered as important as cultivating good taste, and the landscape garden played an important role in this regard. Music, literature, painting, and drama were all played out on the lawn where they could be seen (fig. 6.12). It didn't matter if family members excelled at these gentle arts; simply pursuing them set families securely in a cultured class.

Greater leisure time also allowed families purposefully to groom their social standing. Each season was marked by frantic displays intended to impress the right people, so no setting seemed more conspicuous than the lawn or garden. Receptions, recitals, and tea parties (fig. 6.13) were precisely planned to convey the proper image. Avid social climbers seemed comforted by the thought that palatial grounds and extravagant entertaining could dispel the stigma of more humble beginnings.

As the cost of garden making decreased, and the amount of leisure time increased, public interest in gardening as a hobby showed a corresponding rise. No longer was the art of landscape gardening exclusively reserved for the wealthy. Anyone could try to work in an artistic spirit, even though he or she could not rival the artist's skill. Therefore amateurs, rather than professionals, can be credited with planning and planting the ornamental gardens and grounds around many middle-class homes.

To these Americans, the garden was much more than an artistic arrangement of plants, ornament, and architecture. They believed that garden toil was wholesome and uplifting, bringing them physical and spiritual benefits which would not be purchased by hiring a gardener. These sentiments were frequently expressed by men, who turned to gardening as a remedy for the stresses encountered at the office or factory.

American women turned to gardening too, but for different reasons (fig. 6.3). At first, gardening simply represented an extension of the roles women already played in the home. Just as one would nurture young children, so too, could one care for tender seedlings, diligently creating the conditions that would make them thrive. In the minds of many Americans, this analogy was so sound that mothers often fostered an interest in gardening for their own offspring, believing that garden tasks taught lessons about life. By following mother's example with miniature garden tools of their own, children learned patience, responsibility, and pride of accomplishment, together with the cyclic rhythms of nature.

In other ways, gardening satisfied needs that were left unfulfilled in the nineteenth-century home. Gardening as a hobby enabled women to escape the confines of the house for fresh air and exercise. In *Gardening By Myself,* written especially for women, Anna Warner commented on the restorative power of gardening: you could "forget how tired you were, while tying up pinks bowed down with only the weight of their own loveliness."[3] Gardening also gave women, who were frequently isolated by family responsibilities, the opportunity for social interaction. Through garden clubs, women could trade treasured plants, share practical experiences, and review the most recent gardening advice to appear in the home journals.

Looking back on the gardens of the Gilded Age, we see that income may have affected the extent of the garden one could develop and maintain, but the benefits of gardening were not limited to the wealthy. Science, industry, and technology had revolutionized garden making, so it was well within the reach of most Americans. Furthermore, amateur gardeners—men, women and children alike—seemed compensated for their efforts by improved physical and spiritual well-being. Thus, the pleasures of planting could be enjoyed by all.

By the close of the nineteenth century, ornamental gardens served less as an indicator of social status, and more as a reflection of personal interest and commitment. The beauty of a garden may have been fleeting, but for many, it was well worth the sacrifice of time, money, and effort.

6.1 Mr. Adam in Joseph C. Burritt's Garden, Ithaca, New York, c. 1865
Collection of the DeWitt Historical Society of Tompkins County, Ithaca, New York

Landscape gardening was a little-known occupation in America until the mid-nineteenth century. A chronicler of trades and professions noted in 1837 that, "In Europe, the professed gardeners constitute a large class of the population. They are employed either in their own gardens, or in those of the wealthy, who engage them by the day or year. There are some who devote their attention to this business in this country; but these are chiefly from the other side of the Atlantic. In our Southern states, the rich assign one of their slaves to the garden."[4]

Although he may never have had the benefit of formal education and training in horticulture, Mr. Adam seems eminently proud to be photographed in the upstate New York garden where he worked. He poses with a spading fork, an implement used to dig up borders and around trees because its tines would not injure the roots of existing plantings. Other essential tools of his trade might have included a watering can, hoe, spade, rake, trowel for transplanting, a short-handled sickle and a long-handled scythe for trimming grass. Then, as today, maintaining a garden was not easy. Garden tasks, observed one experienced cultivator, required "a cast-iron back with a hinge in it."[5]

6.2 Gardener in the Garden of H. B. Gibson, 46 North Main Street, Canandaigua, New York, c. 1870 *(Top left, page 119)*
Collection of the Ontario County Historical Society, Canandaigua, New York

The garden of H. B. Gibson in Canandaigua dates from 1822, but has retained its geometrical form, edgings of boxwood, and mingled perennial plantings until 1870 when this photograph was taken. The statuary is stone rather than cast iron, suggesting that it too was an early feature of the garden. Figures in peasant costume were favorite subjects in eighteenth-century British gardens, but less commonly seen in America. Therefore, it is possible that this fine example was imported from England, rather than crafted in this country. A note inscribed on the reverse of this photograph reveals that all statuary faced the porch to please Mrs. Gibson.

Almost resembling a statue himself, the Gibson's gardener pauses from his daily duties to be photographed. He is sensibly outfitted in overalls and boots, and carries a metal watering can and wooden bucket for tending his plantings.

6.3 Amateur Gardener at "Sonnenberg," Canandaigua, New York, 1864
Collection of Sonnenberg Gardens, Canandaigua, New York

This amateur gardener, possibly Mary Clark Thompson, is cultivating her small circular flower bed, one of the most essential garden operations. "The secret of neatness and economy in summer culture of a garden, is to stir the ground often. It is a trifling task to destroy an acre of weeds, if you take them half an inch high; but a very laborious undertaking to get them subdued, if they once are allowed to make strong roots and leaves of full size."[6]

The motivations for gardening in nineteenth-century society were many, and therefore, the activity was sanctioned for men, women, and children alike. Some considered gardening to be morally uplifting. Leisure time spent gardening left little opportunity to frequent the betting parlors or saloons. Others regarded it as a healthy and enjoyable form of exercise. "Planting and gardening supply a fund of entertainment, the most lasting and reasonable of any occupation in this life, pleasures not to be purchased."[7] Finally, gardening was considered by members of the middle and upper classes to be cultured and refined. Although dirt farmers and laboring men may have had little time or energy for ornamental gardening, "yet such is the laudable taste of the fair daughters of America . . . that there are but comparatively few, that do not take an interest in a flower garden."[8]

6.4 Gentleman Posing with Lawnmower. Unidentified Residence, possibly Ithaca, New York, c. 1870
Collection of the Geneva Historical Society, Geneva, New York

Neat lawns became a common sight in America only after mechanical lawnmowers. "These lawn mowers are a real blessing, for not one in ten-thousand can cut a lawn properly with a scythe, and therefore, our lawns, before the introduction of these mowers, always looked wretched."[9] The machine pictured in the lower right of the photograph was the type recommended for general use. It probably cut a swath between fifteen and eighteen inches wide, and cost about twenty-five dollars. Homeowners could also invest in narrower mowers, which were easier to manipulate for trimming turf edgings.

6.5, 6.6 Gardeners and Garden Tasks at "Sonnenberg," Canandaigua, New York, c. 1887
Collection of the Ontario County Historical Society, Canandaigua, New York

When gardening became too ambitious a task for nineteenth-century homeowners, they had to rely on the services of professional horticulturists and landscape gardeners. Sonnenberg, the F. F. Thompson estate in Canandaigua, required a whole retinue of workers to care for the extensive gadens which graced the property.

The gardeners at Sonnenberg used the most up-to-date horticultural methods available. When plans required a stand of mature trees, each could be painstakingly transplanted from other parts of the property. The gardeners also maintained an extensive conservatory and palm house, which provided both the residence and gardens with an abundant supply of flowers and foliage. Frederick Ferris Thompson, wearing a business suit and top hat, is flanked by his employees in this garden portrait. His forty-room summer residence is faintly visible in the background of the view.

6.7 Gardens and Greenhouse at Lunatic Asylum, Utica, New York, c. 1880
Collection of The Oneida Historical Society at Utica, New York

The extensive gardens and greenhouse around this hospital suggest the amount of resources put toward ornamental horticulture by public and private institutions during the latter half of the nineteenth century. Motivation for this embellishment seems to have been twofold. Social reformers were convinced that the quality of the physical environment affected the well-being of the patients. As a result, administrators sought to improve the appearance of their institutions and grounds in an effort to create more supportive settings for residence and rehabilitation. Few features made a greater visual impact than the flower garden.

In addition, gardening as an activity was advocated for good health. "The proofs are apparent everywhere that garden operations are conducive to health and longevity. . . . The growing and the watching of the great variety of plants gives a healthy tone to the mind, while the physical labor demanded by cultivation takes care of the body."[10] By receiving training in the principles and practices of ornamental horticulture, patients could benefit from the physical exercise, take pride in their accomplishments, and perhaps, market their newly-learned skills in the community as hired garden laborers.

6.8 Garden Labor and Leisure, Unidentified Family Group, Albany, New York, c. 1870
Collection of the McKinney Library, Albany Institute of History and Art, Albany, New York

This portrait of a rural family in the 1870s is instructive for its typicality, rather than its uniqueness. Despite the availability of specialy designed "garden" furniture, family members are assembled on the lawn with household pieces, probably pulled from a parlor or a porch to fulfill a temporary role in the garden. Garden literature makes no mention of this practice, but it is commonly seen in historical photographs. The implication is that many families still considered furniture designed for garden use to be a luxury that they could not afford. An 1872 catalog lists a rustic chair for $9.50, costing the average wage-earner more than half a week's salary. A settee for two at $13.00 would take over a week to earn.[11]

Nevertheless, what this family did not spend for comfort, they invested in garden maintenance. The cast-iron roller at right was essential for leveling lawns, roads, and walks after heaving winter frosts, and the settling of spring and summer rains. The fact that they chose to document this article in their family portrait suggests that they placed a high value on landscape and garden tasks.

6.9 Croquet Scene on the Lawn at "Rose Hill," Geneva, New York, c. 1890
Collection of the Geneva Historical Society, Geneva, New York

In this photograph, four children and a young woman play croquet as their elders look on. Croquet was the first outdoor game which families could play together, because it required strategy and skill rather than strength. Therefore, no player had an unfair advantage.

Croquet had its origins in a thirteenth-century French game called "paille maille." By the nineteenth century it reached England and eventually America. "Of all the epidemics that have swept our land, the swiftest and most infectious is croquet."[12]

The American version differed slightly from its British prototype in the number of pegs and wickets used, but the object of the game remained the same. Players or teams drove wooden balls through a series of wire arches using long handled mallets. Each player got two balls and had to complete the course with both balls to win. The game was complicated by the fact that players could strike opponents' balls out of play, making it harder for them to reach their goal. This croquet court was informally arranged in the shape of a figure eight. The vine-covered stump planter in the foreground marks "home peg," the beginning and end point of the course.

6.10 Outfitted for Lawn Tennis, C. F. Wickwire Residence, Cortland, New York, c. 1895
Collection of The 1890 House, Cortland, New York

These young ladies and gentlemen were outfitted for an afternoon of lawn tennis, evidently a much different style of play than the strenuous, competitive game we know today. They are posing in a "portable tent," a cast-iron settee topped with a canvas awning, which was available by catalog as early as the 1870s. "The canvass [*sic*] . . . is a complete protector from the sun and rain at all hours of the day, is easily raised and lowered by pulling a cord attached to the roller above."[13] Other household chairs were temporarily pressed into service on the lawn.

When tennis was first introduced at the Staten Island Cricket Club in 1874, its purpose was purely recreational. It was not too active, required some skill, and was enjoyed by men and women alike.[14] Consequently, the popularity of tennis was not limited to the resort communities where it was first seen. Prominent families, who summered on the shore or in the mountains, brought the sport home, where it became a status symbol.

Tennis did not simply fulfill social motives. It provided much needed exercise for many nineteenth-century families. As the number of city and suburban dwellers surpassed rural residents, the traditional outlets for physical exertion diminished. Outdoor diversions, like tennis, croquet, or team sports, became imperative for both physical and mental health.[15]

6.11 Tableau Reenacting "The Death of Virginia" According to Del'Sarti, Rochester, New York, 1893
Arnold Family Album, Department of Rare Books and Special Collections, The University of Rochester Library, Rochester, New York

This photograph tells more about the social function of the homeground than of its design and planting. Here, several young women portray an historical or allegorical theme on the front lawn of a suburban Rochester home. These performances, called tableaux, required participants to strike a pose and remain motionless, often for a considerable period of time. The audience was supposed to react with astonishment at the likeness of these "living statues" to an actual sculptural or painted group.

In a similar vein, pageants were popular pastimes for nineteenth-century ladies and their daughters. These were slightly more elaborate productions, sometimes with scenery, speaking roles, or processions. Ostensibly, tableaux and pagents reinforced notions of education, culture, and good taste in both participants and audiences, but the underlying appeal was probably a love of spectacle.

6.12 Guests at the Oriental Teahouse at "Sonnenberg," Canandaigua, New York, c. 1910
Collection of the Ontario County Historical Society, Canandaigua, New York

Gardens with a foreign theme or style became very popular at the close of the nineteenth century. By this time, the natural landscape style espoused a half-century earlier by Downing and others seemed ordinary, so fashionable Americans looked elsewhere for sources of inspiration. The wealthy could afford to travel the world, but the rest relied upon expositions and fairs to glimpse the products of foreign cultures. From Maine to California, many tasteful gardens began to take on Italian, French, or Oriental qualities.

In true romantic form, Americans were more interested in evoking the atmosphere or impression of a foreign garden than accurately depicting its organization and detail. Consequently this garden, and others like it, should rightly be called Oriental, for it combined elements from at least three Eastern cultures: Japan, China, and Korea. According to tradition, the predominant plantings were evergreens, suggesting the constancy and endurance of nature. Focal points in the garden included several pedestal lanterns (*tachi-gata*) and the water basin (*tsukubai*) located immediately adjacent to the teahouse, at right. In Japan, the water basin was set close to the ground to induce humility in the guests as they stooped or bent to draw the water. In this case, however, the water basin was placed at waist height on a stone pedestal, perhaps a Western concession to Victorian propriety.

6.13 Horn-Sahs Family Portrait in Arbor, Rochester, New York, c. 1900
Horn-Sahs Papers, Department of Rare Books and Special Collections,
**   The University of Rochester Library, Rochester, New York**

In nineteenth-century America, good taste was not a birthright, like a title or a family crest. It could be acquired through sensitivity, study, and social responsibility. Although the character of the true gentleman was highly evolved, it was, in the spirit of democracy, well within the reach of many a lad from city or country.

With little time or opportunity for ornamental gardening, this immigrant family fabricated a structure that served both as grape arbor and garden house. The perimeter is embellished with potted plants of many kinds: notably a collection of cacti and succulents, including an orchid cactus (*Nopalxochia ackermanii*) in the wooden tub at left. No matter how small it seemed, the effort would have been applauded. In the words of Andrew Jackson Downing, "If landscape gardening, in its proper sense, cannot be applied to the embellishment of the smallest cottage residences in the country, its principles may be studied with advantage, even by him who has only three trees to plant for ornament; and we hope no one will think his grounds too small, to feel willing to add something to the general amount of beauty in the country."[16]

6.14 Gardener at William Andrus Property, Ithaca, New York, c. 1865
Collection of DeWitt Historical Society of Tompkins County, Ithaca, New York

Until the last quarter of the nineteenth century, the profession of horticulture had not attracted many native-born Americans. Critics speculated that, despite its growing complexity, the position did not have the status nor the salary to compete successfully for the interests of young men. To be a good gardener required more than skill; it demanded observation, energy, foresight, and enthusiasm.[17] All too often, the general public considered talented gardeners in the same class with mere garden laborers, "the clodhopper and the wheelbarrow trundler."

Employers had to share the blame for the poor quality of garden labor in America, for few were able to detect mistakes in the routine operations of the fruit, vegetable, or flower garden. A master gardener in 1853 advised, "those who possess gardening establishments [should] begin to acquire a more practical knowledge of such things, so as to be able the more readily to detect the ignorance that is too often practiced upon them. A good gardener will never fear his employer being acquainted with the detail of his work; for if his operations are correct, they will the more readily be seen and appreciated."[18]

Photographic Portraits of Five New York State Gardens

OST of the historical photographs in *Gardens of the Gilded Age* are singular views of New York State gardens and homegrounds. For some, these photographs were purposeful attempts to capture the ephemeral beauty of the landscape and garden. For others, the landscape features were secondary, serving only as backdrops or settings for the subject. Nevertheless, we study them today with equal interest for the clues they contain about the evolution of American environmental traditions.

On rare occasions, gardens and grounds were more throughly documented—from various viewpoints during a single photographic session, or intermittently over several seasons, years, or decades. Collectively, these photographs can reveal much more about the form, function, style, and material of particular gardens and allow greater insight into the people who created them.

In this final chapter, five New York State properties have been selected for a more detailed interpretation of their history. Judging from their size and the skill with which they were created, these properties were not typical of gardens and homegrounds created in America between 1860 and 1917. In fact, they were largely the products of design professionals or talented amateurs. Nevertheless, they illustrate what average Americans were striving to achieve, on a smaller scale with more limited resources, on their own homegrounds. They also reiterate the themes common to many American gardens and homegrounds during the second half of the nineteenth century.

During the Gilded Age, romanticism emerged as a dominant influence on American gardens, resulting in designed landscapes which imitated natural scenery. Two distinguished examples of the natural style of landscape gardening were Cottage Lawn in Oneida (figs. 7.23–7.25) and Renwick-Yates Castle in Syracuse (figs. 7.1–7.10). Both residences were designed by prominent American architects in the Gothic style, but this is where their similarity ends. The design of the landscape garden, in each case, responded uniquely to the character of the site itself.

Despite the widespread popularity of the natural style, interest in neoclassical styles persisted throughout the nineteenth century. At Lorenzo (figs. 7.11–7.17), where members of the same Cazenovia family resided for several generations, both house and garden had formal plans with symmetry being the chief characteristic. Gradually, as times and tastes changed, the garden was modified, but always in keeping with the traditional geometric framework of the original design.

If Lorenzo evolved in the neoclassical tradition, then Box Hill (figs. 7.18–7.22), the Long Island residence of architect Stanford White, was a reinterpretation of the same formal influences. The original frame farmhouse, which lacked the history and elegance of more celebrated examples of early American architecture, was enlarged and embellished in the Colonial Revival style. Its geometry was extended to the landscape as well, where an old-fashioned formal garden, bordered with boxwood, was created to complete the setting.

Nineteenth-century Americans not only looked to the past, but to foreign cultures for inspiration in garden-making. Mary Clark Thompson of Canandaigua collected gardens like others collected plants. Her extraordinary summer estate, Sonnenberg (figs. 7.26–7.33), featured more than a dozen separate gardens, each with a different cultural or aesthetic theme. Although inspired by France, England, Italy, and the Orient, these gardens were more evocative than authentic, and can be appreciated today as uniquely American adaptations.

The gardens of the Gilded Age evolved at a time when America was seeking her own identity in a rapidly changing world. Nostalgic for the past, yet eagerly anticipating the future, Americans sought to resolve this dichotomy through design in architecture, decorative arts, and landscape gardening. During this period, garden professionals took on more specialized roles: seed and nurserymen supplied plants, horticulturists re-created the conditions that would make them thrive, and landscape architects arranged them in a harmonious composition. At the same time, interest in gardens and gardening spread from the owners of large estates to average Americans with a simple desire to improve their surroundings. Consequently, the gardens created during this period were a curious mixture of art and industry, style and taste, imitation and originality, subtlety and spectacle.

The historical photographs in *Gardens of the Gilded Age* illustrate the tremendous diversity which existed among American gardens during the last century, gardens which many simply refer to as "Victorian." Composed of exotic plants, and arranged in an unusual manner, they now seem foreign to many of us, perhaps even a bit bizarre, or at least "old-fashioned." However, the gardens of the Gilded Age were considered to be modern and forward-thinking during their day; and the nineteenth-century homeground went far beyond being merely a tasteful arrangement of garden ornament, or just an extensive collection of horticultural treasures and elaborate floral embellishments. If, for a moment, we can put aside our own "good taste," our twentieth-century values, and our veil of nostalgia, and look beyond the flower beds and gazebos, we will begin to see the gardens of the Gilded Age in a different light—as products of a particular time, place, and personality, and as reflections of life in America during the nineteenth century.

From this broader perspective, it is clear that the garden had become a half-way world between the nineteenth-century family and society: a center for domesticity and leisure, an equal partner to the parlor, a counterbalance to the world of work, and for a few, a social stage. Although most nineteenth-century gardens have long ago disappeared and their plants have withered and died, historic photographs like these enable us to share in the experience, so we may better understand the gardens of the last century and the people who created them.

Renwick-Yates Castle, Syracuse, New York
A Curious Mixture of Rustic and Refined

For nearly one hundred years, Renwick-Yates Castle stood atop the "Syracuse Hill," a tribute to the affluence and taste of its owners, and the romantic vision of the architect for which it was named. Today, along Irving Avenue, one can find only remnants of the crenellated wall which once surrounded the property.

The initial inspiration for the Castle, built between 1852 and 1854, belonged to Cornelius Tyler Longstreet, a Syracuse businessman whose aspirations were exceeded only by his wealth. After making a fortune as a clothier in Syracuse and New York City, he sought to build a suitable residence for himself and his family. The site he chose was a hillside property overlooking the city, but far from the fashionable neighborhoods of his Syracuse associates.

To design his residence, Longstreet commissioned James Renwick, Jr. (1818–95), a young, well-bred and well-educated architect from New York City, whose work was already widely acclaimed. Renwick's first prestigious project had been Grace Church in New York, a Gothic Revival structure built between 1843 and 1846. Almost immediately, he went on to design the now familiar "Castle" headquarters of the Smithsonian Institution in Washington, D.C. Its Norman or castellated Gothic style was the prototype for the Renwick-Yates Castle in Syracuse.

As in the Smithsonian Castle, Renwick used architectural details reminiscent of twelfth-century Europe. The castle in Syracuse featured low roofs concealed with a line of battlements cut out of solid parapet walls, pointed and square-headed windows, and massive octagonal towers which projected skyward, giving the building an irregular silhouette. The castellated Gothic style was even used for the outbuildings: barn, tenant's house, billiard alley, ice house, and gate lodge.

Today, it is difficult to appreciate how unique this structure would have seemed to the residents of Syracuse in 1854. Since upstate New York was fairly conservative, the prevailing taste of the day was still Greek Revival, and even the Gothic cottage was considered progressive. Andrew Jackson Downing, who approved of its romantic allusions, admitted that the castellated Gothic style was well beyond the reach of the average homeowner. "This mode of building is evidently of too ambitious and expensive a kind for a republic, where landed estates are not secured by entail, but divided among the different members of a family. It is, perhaps, also wanting in appropriateness, castles never having been used for defence [sic] in this country. Notwithstanding these objections, there is no very weighty reason why a wealthy proprietor should not erect his mansion in the castellated style, if that style be in unison with his scenery and locality."[1]

For James Renwick, Jr., this last condition seemed to be the key. The prevailing attitude among architects and landscape gardeners was that "the castellated style never appears completely at home except in wild and romantic scenery. . . . To place such a building in this country on a smooth surface in the midst of fertile plains, would immediately be felt to be bad taste by everyone . . ."[2] Although Longstreet's fifteen acres of land might have been small compared to the aristocratic country estates found elsewhere, its location was peerless. Situated on the eastern rise of the Onondaga valley, "the splendid view from the Castle takes in the country range of twenty-five or thirty miles around, in a clear atmosphere, embracing a bird's-eye view of Pompey Hill, seventeen miles distant, and overlooking the entire valley of the Onondaga, with its romantic surroundings."[3] Consequently, the varied topography of the Syracuse site formed a far more appropriate setting for a Norman castle than the comparatively level site of the Smithsonian institution, Renwick's earlier project in Washington.

Exactly who was responsible for the landscape gardening of the Renwick-Yates castle is not clear. Early twentieth-century sources variously attribute the architect himself, and Lewis Redfield, Longstreet's neighbor and father-in-law. In any case, the grounds were laid out in the natural style, to correspond with the irregular character of the architecture. This was in conformity with the principles which Downing had elucidated in his *Treatise on the Theory and Practice of Landscape Gardening* only ten years earlier.

After entering by the Gate Lodge at the northeast corner of the site, visitors and family crossed a gully or ravine by way of a rustic wooden bridge. The carriage drive led to the west façade, which was the principal entrance to the residence, and then on to the ornamental grounds, billiard alley and stables. Plantings were done in an equally naturalistic way, with picturesque deciduous trees and evergreens intermixed on the lawns near the residence. In the beginning, embellishment was probably kept to a minimum, with the rustic mode predominating. Later, the grounds became punctuated with ornament and architecture of every description.

The Longstreet family lived on the hill until 1866, when the isolation they felt from business and family friends compelled them to move back to the city. They exchanged their castle for the James Street residence of Alonzo Chester Yates, to which a considerable cash settlement was added. Like Longstreet, Yates was a prominent Syracuse businessman and clothier, but his fortune came instead from the manufacture of uniforms sold to the Federal government during the Civil War. Yates spent the final years of the conflict in Europe, where he undoubtedly acquired a taste for the Old World. Shortly after his return, he acquired Renwick Castle for his residence.

Before long, the Renwick Castle became known as Yates Castle, the name being only one of numerous changes during the Yates residency. In general, the character of the grounds changed from a rural, rustic mode to a more suburban, embellished style. "The spacious and well laid out grounds attached, embrace some fifteen acres, eleven of which compose the ornamental grounds of the castle and its surroundings, with four acres devoted to a floral and vegetable garden, including conservatory and greenhouse. The grounds of the Castle contain a lavish display of ornaments, in statuary, summer houses, rustic arches and seats, gilded lamps, reflecting globes of quicksilver mounted upon pedestals, and a wealth of the choicest flowers and fruit, and rarest plants and exotics, in keeping with so grand a private summer retreat. A beautiful Italian Garden, terraced and planted with varieties of grape vines and foreign exotics, with a gravelled roadway running along the bottom of an extensive ravine spanned by a rustic bridge, claims the attention of the visitor upon first entering the grounds, and attracts the eye in connection with the other romantic scenery before him, and spouting fountains of crystal jets, with their rare shells and corals, give the idea of a grotto in some fairy or other enchanted spot."[4] These changes left the castle grounds a curious mixture of rustic and rich, a combination considered distasteful by purists, but nevertheless adulated by the public.

During the 1870s, Yates Castle was renowned as a local attraction. Not only was it the scene of elegant parties, but the grounds were opened regularly for visitors, a gesture considered by tourists to be exceptionally generous. Yates Castle also figured prominently in photographic views—postcards and stereoviews—of Syracuse and its surroundings. However, the death of Alonzo Yates in 1880 resulted in the gradual decline of the property and of the Yates fortune, at the hands of his son, Alonzo Yates, Jr. In 1898, the furnishings of Yates Castle were dispersed at auction, and Yates's wife and son retired in voluntary exile to France, never returning to Syracuse.

By the turn of the century, maintaining Renwick-Yates Castle was beyond the means of even the most wealthy Syracusans. It continued to survive as a private institution; first, as the Syracuse Classical School and subsequently, as department offices and classrooms for Syracuse University's School of Journalism. Renwick-Yates Castle was razed for the construction of the State University of New York, Upstate Medical College at Syracuse.

7.1 Renwick Castle, East Façade, Probably 1866–67
Collection of the Onondaga Historical Association, Syracuse, New York

Renwick Castle illustrates many characteristics of the picturesque mode in landscape gardening. The residence in the castellated Gothic style has striking forms with bold projections, deep shadows, and irregular outlines. Likewise, the landscape shows intricacy and variety in its planning and planting. Each was designed to complement the other to create a complete composition.

7.2 Rustic Bridge on Castle Grounds, Probably 1866–67
Collection of the Onondaga Historical Association. Syracuse, New York

7.3 Renwick Castle Bridge, c. 1860
Collection of The Library of Congress, Washington, D.C.

This rustic bridge, one of the original features of the Renwick Castle grounds, allowed carriages and pedestrians to cross a small ravine near the entrance to the property. Built of timbers, it was very much in keeping with the rugged and natural character of the original landscape garden.

7.4 West Entrance of Renwick-Yates Castle, c. 1878
Collection of the Onondaga Historical Association, Syracuse, New York

In the picturesque landscape, rustic work was considered to be the only appropriate ornament for areas near the residence, and in the more frequented parts of the grounds. These triple-tiered planters were simply fabricated of branches and twigs. Their material and construction recall the rustic bridge at the entrance to the property.

7.5 Inside View of the Gate Lodge at Renwick-Yates Castle, c. 1877
Collection of the Onondaga Historical Association, Syracuse, New York

Alonzo Yates added a coat-of-arms and this imposing black and gilt gate, built to resemble long spears or pikes. Unfortunately, the classical statuary in the foreground detracts from, rather than enhances, the medieval impression.

7.6 Italian Garden from the Rustic Bridge, c. 1878

7.7 Italian Garden from the Ravine, c. 1878
Collection of the Onondaga Historical Association, Syracuse, New York

Views of the Italian Garden from the rustic bridge made the first impression on visitors to the castle. No longer a rugged ravine as in the earlier photograph, the hillsides have been terraced and planted with ornamental trees and shrubs, clipped to enhance their formal appearance. Along the upper levels, grape vines supported on ladder-like trellises rimmed the garden. On the opposite side, flanking the bridge, were stairways which ascended to the ornamental grounds nearer the castle. Classical vases and statuary provided the artistic focal points. Beyond the crenelated wall which marked the boundary of the Longstreet-Yates property was Syracuse University. The Second Empire style structure in the background is the Hall of Languages, the first academic building constructed on the hill.

7.8 Greenhouse or Conservatory at Renwick-Yates Castle, c. 1877
Collection of the Onondaga Historical Association, Syracuse, New York

Alonzo Yates added this small greenhouse to the ornamental grounds near the castle. In keeping with the Gothic style of the residence, the greenhouse had pointed arches and an octagonal cupola, but was constructed of wood and glass. Its cruciform plan allowed the gardener to select the proper exposure for any kind of plant. However, beyond its functional flexibility, it was highly ornamental. Note the cast-iron roof cresting, the polychrome slates, and figure of "Victory" atop the cupola.

7.9 Gothic Summerhouse, Renwick-Yates Castle, c. 1878
Collection of the Onondaga Historical Association, Syracuse, New York

The octagonal shape of the principal tower at the Renwick-Yates Castle was reiterated in the grounds with the small, eight-sided summerhouse. Again, the details were Gothic — pointed arches, tracery, pinnacles — but the effect was airy and light, in contrast to the fortified appearance of the castle. This structure was meant to be a cool summer retreat. Lath screens provided shade within; low benches lined four of the eight sides. Its site on the hillside southwest of the residence would have caught every available summer breeze. Garden ornament provided an elegant foreground for views from the summerhouse. The classical vases are identical to those flanking the stairway into the Italian Garden. The statue is of carved or cast stone, not necessarily imported.

7.10 The Chapel, Renwick-Yates Castle Grounds, c. 1878
Collection of the Onondaga Historical Association, Syracuse, New York

Located just southwest of the principal entrance to the Castle, the Chapel was one of the most unusual features of the castle grounds. Since it was barely large enough to enter, it more closely resembled a shrine or memorial. As in all the outbuildings, the organization and detail were Gothic.

Other Photographs of Renwick-Yates Castle
2.3   The Ravine at Renwick-Yates Castle, Syracuse, New York, c. 1887.
4.7   Rustic retreat at Renwick-Yates Castle, Syracuse, New York, c. 1870.

"Lorenzo," Cazenovia, New York
The Persistence of Earlier Traditions

Historical garden photographs of the nineteenth century are filled with examples of mass-produced garden ornament, modern horticultural methods, and new technological developments. Less common is the garden in which an older style persists, not from neglect, but as a result of conscious design decisions which respected earlier traditions. Such was the case at Lorenzo, the Federal Style residence of the Lincklaen-Ledyard family. The garden retained its original geometry through the period of romantic naturalism, until its formality was again appreciated during the Colonial Revival era (1870–1920). Today, Lorenzo is an historic site, operated by the New York State Office of Parks, Recreation and Historic Preservation, Central Region.

At first, Lorenzo was distinguished only by the taste of its owner and the potential of its site. A visitor to Cazenovia related his impressions of the place in 1806 before the development of the house and grounds. "Walked with Mr. Lincklaen to see where he intends building, which is on a gentle elevation, about twenty rods from the turnpike, thirty or forty rods from the east end of the lake, to which the land is nearly level or very gentle descent. He will have a very fine prospect, the lake in front, town to the right, handsomely rising ground to the left, and behind, his farm, extending to the Canaserago main stream on which are some fine flat lands. It will afford an opportunity of laying out the pleasure grounds to much advantage, and will be one of the most beautifull [*sic*] seats in the state."[5]

For his residence, Colonel John Lincklaen built a fashionable two-story brick structure in the Federal style. It featured a low-pitched roof surmounted by a pediment and balustrade, and a smooth façade punctuated evenly with windows. The principal entrance was in the center of the north façade facing the lake. As with many Federal style residences, the door was ornamented above with an elliptical fan light and flanked by slender side lights.

The garden was planned with the same formality as the residence. Although no detailed drawings of the original garden have survived, maps indicate that it was sited immediately south of the residence on approximately one acre of land. A wooden fence or hedge probably separated it from the surrounding agricultural land. The central walk ran north and south extending from the main hall of the mansion. "In eight squares this garden was first laid out, with three rectangular areas on the side, all intersected with right angled walks, and filled with beds of vegetables and edgings of flowers . . ."[6] The result was a very direct physical and visual relationship between house and garden, a tradition in America since gardening began.

By the time nephew Ledyard Lincklaen acquired Lorenzo in 1843, garden styles had begun to change. Andrew Jackson Downing had already published his influential *Treatise on the Theory and Practice of Landscape Gardening,* and Lincklaen added it to his personal library. Yet, despite knowledge of new principles and practices of landscape gardening, Ledyard Lincklaen respected his garden's heritage and planted in accordance with the older style.

Changes to the garden by Ledyard Lincklaen revealed his personal interest in pomology and botany. Fruit trees—apples, pears, and plums—were not restricted to the orchard, but introduced into the formal garden to accent the corners of the squares. Some of these may have replaced earlier plantings by John Lincklaen. During the middle decades of the nineteenth century, references to growing vegetables within the garden enclosure ceased. Instead, historical photographs show panels of turf accented in the centers with single specimens of Norway spruce (*Picea abies*). Lincklaen also added evergreens at the perimeter of the garden: white pines (*Pinus strobus*), hemlocks (*Tsuga canadensis*), Norway spruces, white cedars (*Thuya occidentalis*), and Scotch pines (*Pinus sylvestris*).

Ledyard Lincklaen was also responsible for introducing several ornamental features in the garden. He built a small wooden playhouse in the northeast quadrant of the garden near the residence. His daughter Helen whimsically called it "Apple Tree Cottage." Ledyard Lincklaen also placed a sundial atop a boulder at the center of the formal garden, to mark the intersection of the principal paths.

It wasn't until the third quarter of the nineteenth century that the unity and harmony of America's earliest gardens were again appreciated by the general public. With unprecedented patriotic enthusiasm, Americans embraced their own history, and interpreted it in the interiors, architecture, and gardens of the Colonial Revival. Lorenzo, continuously occupied by members of the same family since 1807, had a larger claim to authenticity than most other nineteenth-century homegrounds. A visitor to Lorenzo about 1890 acknowledged the popularity of the Colonial Revival and commented on its appropriateness. "The revival of these old fashioned gardens has become something of a fad among individuals. The place for them is before or behind an old fashioned house. The writer visited one this summer, upon which a great deal of time, money, loving thought and knowledge had been expended . . ."[7]

By this time, the youthful mistress of Apple Tree Cottage had become the first lady of Lorenzo itself. The wife of a well-respected politician, Helen Lincklaen Fairchild steadfastly carried on the garden traditions initiated by her father and great-uncle. Descriptions of the garden during the 1890s reveal the persistence of garden features introduced a generation or two earlier. "The house is a century old, very large and filled with ancient furniture. From the wide hall that runs through the center, the garden is framed like a picture by the door to the back piazza—a path leads straight away broken only in mid-distance by an old sundial on a mound. Norway [spruces] stand like sentinels on either side in the foreground and far away the path terminates in an image of six foot hedge of evergreens, above which pines again raise their heads.[8] On each side of the path, for the whole distance are beds crowded with all sorts of hardy flowers, perennials and annuals. There are no geometrical patterns [that is, floral bedding]. There is no art, that art does not conceal; and when one has reached the paths end and walked through the little maze of tall hedge one comes on a pine walk, a cathedral aisle, carpeted with pine needles closely walled by the pines columns and trunks and winding in a half circle, that leads around the garden and back again to the house."[9]

The visitor went on to suggest that the garden and residence were alike in their dignity and modesty, and the same could be said of the personality of the owner. "After a long, cool walk, full of enchantingly changing views, the mistress with her tranquil face, her old fashioned silver ornaments fit perfectly into the scene."[10]

Unlike her father and great-uncle, Mrs. Fairchild seemed to be more interested in floriculture than in pomology or botany. The volumes she added to the library at Lorenzo included many popular titles: *Sun-Dials and Roses of Yesterday* (1902) by Alice Morse Earle, *Old Fashioned Flowers* (1905) by Maurice Maeterlinck, *A Woman's Hardy Garden* (1907) and *The Practical Flower Garden* (1911) by Helena Rutherford Ely, and *The American Flower Garden* (1909) by Neltje Blanchan.

According to an article which appeared in *Country Life in America* (1902), Mrs. Fairchild's flower borders featured old-fashioned favorites, "those that like to grow there, for the climate is severe and there are no greenhouses to protect tender and unwilling kinds." The author went on to list a great many perennials, together with flowering vines and shrubs. The nostalgic terms in which these old-fashioned flowers were described suggest that they were considered uncommon at the turn of the century, vestiges of flower gardening in an age too remote for most to remember. ". . . Valerian, the 'garden heliotrope' of our mother's garden—does not the scent of it mean something to you yet? fine old single and double peonies; tiger lilies—you can find them persisting still about the rotten foundations of long-abandoned New England farmhouses; the yellow and white day-lilies (*Hemerocallis* and *Funkia*); herbaceous spireas; the old cowslip primroses and polyanthuses; the gas-plant or dictamnus; veronica; bunches of old-time iris; sweet williams, as careless as ever they were in your boyhood; the little stone-cress or sedum, rambling over the edges and into the crannies; feverfew; Oswego tea or monarda; ragged robin and his kind; perennial phlox; plume poppy or bocconia; larkspurs; the old blue and white spiderworts or tradescantias; Jacob's ladder or polemonium; foxgloves. From the woods there are colonies of false Solomon's Seal and bloodroot, clumps of ferns and stately plants of the baneberry or actea, and the Alleghany vine or adlumia, clambering over the bushes. Under the trees is a carpet of the English ivy—as one sees it so much in Europe and in parts of California, and yet we despair to grow it because it winter-kills when trained on buildings. One sees familiar old shrubs, too: flowering locust (*Robinia hispida*), Harison's yellow rose, calycanthus or sweet-scented shrub, double spirea, honeysuckles, mockorange or philadelphus, and a wealth of lilacs. The Crimson Rambler rose also thrives; and also actinidia, the climbing Rosa setigera, Clematis paniculata, and other things of more recent time. Lavender stands the climate when once well rooted. The common wild grape is used to advantage as an arbor cover. And there are pinks!"[11] These old-fashioned flowers were offered, not necessarily as an indictment against the ribbon or carpet bedding which was popular at the time, but as a hardy alternative to tender annuals, "as a source of education to those who wish to make the best and easiest garden in the world."[12]

By 1917, taste in landscape gardening had gone full circle. The ideal garden in America was described in terms which even Colonel John Lincklaen would have understood a century earlier. "The ideal garden picks up the lines of the house and continues them in its own, for the formalistic garden is of the house and its belongings; it dispenses with the roof and modifies the walls to let in sunshine and air, and substitutes flowers that are alive for the painted ones of silks and chintzes. In enlarging the scale of the house, however, it does not lose the intimate feeling of a living room, but merely adds to it the free spirit of outdoors."[13]

7.11 "Lorenzo," Residence of John Lincklaen, Cazenovia, New York, c. 1860
New York State Office of Parks, Recreation, and Historic Preservation, Bureau of
Historic Sites, Lorenzo State Historic Site, Central Region

John Lincklaen built this Federal style residence overlooking Cazenovia Lake in 1806. The formal treatment of the façade also carried over to the design of the grounds. A large lawn with ornamental plantings separated the mansion from the road. A symmetrical, horseshoe-shaped carriage drive approached the residence from the northwest and northeast. As with many country estates of the late eighteenth century, the formal garden was located at the rear of the residence, related to the architecture with a strong central axis.

7.12 Central Garden Walk and Flower Borders at "Lorenzo," c. 1902
New York State Office of Parks, Recreation, and Historic Preservation, Bureau of
Historic Sites, Lorenzo State Historic Site, Central Region

The main axis of the formal garden ran north-south along a central path which extended
from the main hallway of the residence. Lateral walks further divided the garden into
eight rectangular parterres. By mid-century, these became turf panels, accented with
specimen trees and bordered with narrow beds of perennial plants. This early summer
photograph illustrates the peonies in bloom.

7.13 North Border Walk Looking West from Central Path, c. 1865
New York State Office of Parks, Recreation, and Historic Preservation, Bureau of
Historic Sites, Lorenzo State Historic Site, Central Region

By 1865, when the first garden photographs were taken, the evolution of the garden was
already apparent. Tradition persisted in the northwest parterre, which featured a venerable fruit tree, probably a remnant of the original garden planned and planted by John
Lincklaen in 1808. Over a half-century old, its aged trunk had to be supported by poles.
By comparison, the northeast parterre, across the central path, featured a child's playhouse (fig. 4.5). Its name, "Apple Tree Cottage," is reminiscent perhaps, of the tree which
may have originally completed a pair at the entrance of the garden.

7.14 East Lawn of the Formal Garden Looking North, c. 1865
New York State Office of Parks, Recreation, and Historic Preservation, Bureau of
    Historic Sites, Lorenzo State Historic Site, Central Region

Each of the four central parterres in the garden at Lorenzo featured a single Norway spruce (*Picea abies*). In the 1840s when the spruces were planted, they were considered to be a novelty, introduced from northern Europe. As this specimen attests, Norway spruces were prized for their sweeping, feathery branches and graceful form.

7.15 Central Walk Looking North toward the Residence, date unknown
New York State Office of Parks, Recreation, and Historic Preservation, Bureau of
    Historic Sites, Lorenzo State Historic Site, Central Region

The two main axes of the formal garden intersected at a circle of turf about twenty feet in diameter. In 1865, Ledyard Lincklaen placed a sundial here, atop a granite boulder, to serve as a focal point at the center of the garden. In the background to the left of the path is the honeylocust (*Gleditsia triacanthos*) which Lincklaen planted about 1840. Low-lying branches supported by poles created a shady sitting area during the summer months. Garden furniture has been placed in the path for the comfort of the family.

7.16 Central Walk Looking South from Sundial, c. 1880
New York State Office of Parks, Recreation, and Historic Preservation, Bureau of
    Historic Sites, Lorenzo State Historic Site, Central Region

The central path terminated at a bench enframed with an arbor of climbing roses. Mature white pines (*Pinus strobus*), planted between 1854 and 1860, form a dark backdrop, separating the garden from the level land beyond.

7.17 East Border Walk and Hedge, date unknown
New York State Office of Parks, Recreation, and Historic Preservation, Bureau of
    Historic Sites, Lorenzo State Historic Site, Central Region

The perimeter of the garden along the north and east was marked by a wall of evergreens, probably white cedar (*Thuja occidentalis*) in this section. Although hedges were both attractive and functional, this one screened views of the adjacent carriage house.

Other Photographs of Lorenzo
4.5 Helen Fairchild Seated in Front of "Apple Tree Cottage" at Lorenzo, Cazenovia, New York,
        c. 1865
5.2 Flower Garden at Lorenzo, Cazenovia, New York, c. 1865

"Box Hill"
Long Island Residence of Architect Stanford White

Box Hill was the primary residence of famed architect Stanford White from 1884 until his death in 1906. With partners Charles Follen McKim and William Rutherford Mead, he is perhaps best known for designing buildings inspired by renaissance and classical forms. White's talent, however, did not end with architecture, but encompassed landscape architecture and the decorative arts. Box Hill was his creation, shared with his wife, Bessie Smith White, and only son, Lawrence Grant White. It presents a unique opportunity to examine the architect as homeowner, and as a reflection of White's personal tastes and needs.

Box Hill, located at St. James on the North Shore of Long Island, was originally the family farm of Samuel Carman. The simple woodframe dwelling was not significantly different from the other farmhouses which dotted the rural countryside. What made it special, though, was its panoramic view of Stony Brook Harbor. Until the mid-nineteenth century, few people had experienced the scenic beauty of these relatively isolated areas of Long Island. With the coming of the railroad in 1860, however, the rural character was changed dramatically. Waterfront property along the North Shore attracted wealthy tourists from nearby New York City, making Stony Brook Harbor, with its adjacent communities, a popular location for expensive country estates.

Stanford White's motive for acquiring the Carman Farm in 1884 was not simply because the North Shore had become fashionable. The Carman Farm had been a childhood haunt of his wife, Bessie Smith White. Unlike many of their neighbors, Mrs. White was not a nouveau riche newcomer from the city. She was a Long Island native and direct descendant of Richard "Bull" Smith, the seventeenth-century founder of nearby Smithtown. In 1926, she fondly reminisced, "My sisters and I all became famous swimmers, and on hot summer days we used to beg Father to let us take the old gray horse out of the hay field, so we could drive down to the harbor for a swim. It was two-and-a-half miles and we often had to walk, but we scarcely ever missed a day.

"In driving to the harbor just before we reached the Cordwood Path, I used to get out and run across the fields—to look at the view from 'Carman's Hill' and then join the others down the hill at the Harbor, where we had our bath-houses. This view became a passion with me, so much so that later, when I married, my Father told Stanford, he was sure I never would be happy or content to live anywhere else but on top of 'Carman's Hill.' So we bought this hill and after nearly fifty years, I am still living there. It used to be a landmark for the mariners as it was the highest point anywhere around."[14]

The transformation of the Carman farm to Box Hill began in 1884 with White's purchase of the property, and continued through the 1890s. It is difficult to speculate why White decided to renovate the original farmhouse, rather than remove it. Perhaps it was out of professional respect for local building traditions or, like others of his generation, just sentimentality. Whatever the reason, Box Hill assured the continuity of an authentically American architectural style. Like its predecessor, it dominated the rising ground from Stony Brook Harbor.

The first changes at Box Hill were rather conservative. The original ground floor rooms were retained for the dining room and hall. These living spaces were extended with minor alterations to the floor plan. Gradually, however, White made more radical changes, until the original features of the farmhouse were no longer evident. With the addition of ornamented gables, bay windows, and piazzas to the dwelling, and extensive planting, grading, and leveling of the grounds, the Carman farm was eventually transformed to an elegant country residence.

The architectural changes at Box Hill reflect Stanford White's interest in the Neo-Colonial or Colonial Revival mode. As one contemporary writer described it, the cornice and frieze of the entire house are "of the most ornamental Colonial type. . . . At both ends of the entrance hall are old Colonial doorways, with unusually fine leaded glass designs and mouldings covered with ornament."[15] Their inspiration probably dates from a study trip through New England which White took in 1877 with McKim and Mead. Even the name chosen for the estate, Box Hill, suggests a preoccupation with America's colonial heritage. "Box" is the abbreviated term for boxwood, a common edging plant in eighteenth-century gardens. During the last decades of the nineteenth century, after America's centennial celebration, boxwood was considered symbolic of the colonial experience, and of the early American home.

At Box Hill, the geometry of the architecture extends to the grounds, giving a strong organization to an otherwise common landscape. House and garden are linked by a two-tiered terrace carved out of the hillside. The first terrace is simply a sloping grass bank broken by a set of bluestone steps. Below is the garden terrace, bordered by a rubble retaining wall about three feet high. Although its organization is somewhat reminiscent of gardens in colonial America, Stanford White's formal garden shows stylistic influences of Italian Classicism, French Baroque, and more. Continued the writer, "The first portion of the garden forms a geometrical square of four symmetrical beds. These are divided, as are all the beds of the garden in fact, by small white pebbled paths. They encircle a fountain, in the center of which a marble Venus crouches on a shell. A border, a foot high, of the bushiest imaginable box, encloses all the parterres. The center of each of the surrounding beds is marked by one of the magnificent laurel trees, around which grows irregularly a mass of flowers of every description: morning glory, libernum, geraniums, iris, fleurs-de-lis, etc.

"Below these, at a slightly lower level, comes a splendid box hedge, surrounded at various points by its larger clusters, then two larger beds of flowers, and finally, terminating the whole, the pergola, standing out in its shining whiteness against the magnificent background of the wood. This feature could not have been better placed. Not only is it the key-note of the plan of the garden, but it dominates it from every point of view from which it can be seen."[16]

White's lack of a single derivative style is also reflected in the ornament with which he embellished the grounds. "Wherever the position may be a good one, Mr. White has placed a piece of old statuary, sometimes a Greek capital, standing on the lawn between olive-leaved bushes, a row of amphorae against a wall, a rich terra-cotta vase, an ancient carved sarcophagus or finely modelled head upon a marble vase."[17]

White's eclecticism was not limited to garden ornament. It extended to plants as well, particularly the use of exotic specimens in pots and tubs. Historical photographs illustrate laurel and orange trees, pittosporum and pomegranate reminiscent of the gardens in southern Europe. There were green immigrants from other regions too: hydrangeas from South Africa, miniature bonsai trees from Japan, and boxwood in the Dutch tradition, whimsically pruned to look like birds or beasts. Because most could not survive the winters on Long Island, these portable plants were sheltered in the Orangerie, one of numerous outbuildings located south of the residence and formal garden.

Stanford White's garden at Box Hill reflects, above all, his ebullient character. As with architecture, he delighted in pattern, ornament, and embellishment. He also sought inspiration from many sources, both foreign and domestic, past and present, to create gardens and grounds that were intensely personal. In this way, he was like many of his contemporaries. The significant difference, however, was that White did not use landscape elements indiscriminately. He skillfully placed them within the context of the architecture, the garden, the terrace, or the drives—each with a strong order of its own. Consequently, he succeeded where other amateurs and professionals had failed. In the simplest and most straightforward way, geometry gave unity to his composition, and tempered the complicated variety of the details.

7.18 Garden Terrace at "Box Hill," St. James, Long Island, c. 1895

7.19 Pergola at Terminus of Flower Garden, "Box Hill," c. 1895
Collection of the Society for the Preservation of Long Island Antiquities, Setauket, New York

Stanford White's Long Island residence, Box Hill, reveals the freedom with which architects and landscape architects of the late nineteenth century looked to the past and to other cultures to find relevant themes for American design. Here, the architecture of the residence was clearly influenced by the Colonial Revival, but the same cannot be said of the setting. The flower garden, although geometric in organization, featured details borrowed from ancient Greece, Renaissance Italy, and baroque France. According to an article published in *House and Garden* magazine in 1903, the ten Ionic columns of this classical pergola were copied from the Erechtheum in Athens.

7.20 Front Terrace and Drive at "Box Hill," St. James, Long Island, c. 1895

7.21 Rear View of Residence, "Box Hill," St. James, Long Island, c. 1895
Collection of the Society for the Preservation of Long Island Antiquities, Setauket, New York

The verandas and drive at Box Hill were embellished with a curious assortment of plants and ornament: bonsai from Japan, clipped evergreen, orange, and bay trees reminiscent of the gardens of France, and terra-cotta oil jars from Italy. Surprisingly, none of this seemed incongruous to the Victorian frame of mind. Like signatures collected in an autograph book, each element simply suggested another time or place, without requiring an accurate physical reconstruction of the setting.

7.22 The Exedra, "Box Hill," c. 1895
Collection of the Society for the Preservation of Long Island Antiquities, Setauket, New York

This temple-like structure was sited on a small hillock below the residence overlooking Stony Brook Harbor. Ten slender Doric columns formed a circle which supported the entablature and beams. Like the eighteenth-century English noblemen who placed temples within their groves for drama and contrast, Stanford White "animated the horizon" of Stony Brook Harbor by juxtaposing this neoclassical structure with a naturalistic setting.

"Cottage Lawn," Oneida, New York
An Early Example of Residence and Grounds in the Natural Style

Cottage Lawn is a mid-nineteenth century Gothic Revival residence located in Oneida, New York. For nearly one hundred years, it was the home of the Niles Higinbotham family. Today, it serves as a house museum and the headquarters of the Madison County Historical Society.

Niles Higinbotham (1813–90) was the son of Sands Higinbotham, who is credited with founding the village of Oneida. An entrepreneur in merchandising, land speculation, and banking, Niles Higinbotham built Cottage Lawn in 1849, to commemorate his marriage to Miss Eliza Randall (1823–1903) of nearby Manlius, New York. They chose A. J. Davis of New York, one of the most prominent architects of the day, to prepare the plans.

In design and detail, Cottage Lawn is characteristic of the Gothic Revival or "English Cottage" style. When it was constructed, Cottage Lawn's asymmetrical form, pointed arches and tracery designs were highly expressive of "the refined and unostentatious enjoyments of the country."[18] Family tradition suggests that the name "Cottage Lawn" was given to the place by Mrs. Higinbotham, affirming the significance of both residence and grounds to the property owners.

According to garden tastemakers, residences in the Gothic style required landscapes in the "picturesque" mode, preferably a natural woodland setting with old trees, irregular landforms, and abrupt or rocky surfaces. At Cottage Lawn, however, the undeveloped site was relatively flat and probably devoid of any substantial trees, a situation far from ideal. Undoubtedly, the task of creating an appropriate landscape setting for the Higinbotham's cottage became the responsibility of either a professional landscape designer or a skilled amateur.

Family legend attributes the design of the grounds to an anonymous landscape artist from Boston, but to this day archival sources can neither confirm or refute this allegation. References to the grounds do appear in the daybooks of A. J. Davis, documenting that he was responsible for the architectural embellishments. In 1850, he provided the Higinbothams with recommendations for a fence constructed of wood in a Gothic design, with widely spaced pickets and alternating tracery arches. The fence, mounted on a high solid base, was capped by a continuous rail. Davis also designed a hexagonal garden pavilion for Cottage Lawn in 1853. The Gothic structure featured a sharply pointed roof of board-and-batten, coped bargeboards, paired benches, and lattice trellising on two sides. This unique structure remains on the site today, not far from its original location; the Gothic fence, however, was removed during the early decades of the twentieth century.

Historical photographs, maps, and pictorial atlases clearly reveal that the ornamental grounds of Cottage Lawn were laid out according to the "picturesque" mode. Native evergreen trees, whose "spiry-topped" forms complemented chimneys and pointed gables of the residence, were planted in large groves to enframe views of the house. At the same time, these plantings concealed utilitarian features on the site — barns, yards, and outbuildings — and gave a reason, although after the fact, for paths and drives to curve. To unite the structure and setting, native hardwoods and evergreen trees were planted along the drive in front of the residence, achieving a harmonious effect which would have delighted even Downing. Similarly, the judicious use of ornamental trees, like the flowering horse-chestnut (*Aesculus hippocastanum*), offered a rare and beautiful embellishment to the grounds at Cottage Lawn.

It was the expanse of lawn in front of the residence, however, which conveyed a sense of order, neatness, and unity to the scene. Its openness permitted views and vistas through the site and extended the piazza of the cottage into the landscape, while its cool green color created an effective backdrop for colorful beds of flowers, ornamental shrubs, and vines. Equally important, the smooth, velvety surface of the lawn contrasted with the "wild" and "picturesque" character of the nearby evergreen groves. The lawns, together with the shady woodland paths and drives at their margins, offered endless opportunities for enjoying the outdoors: promenades, recreation, relaxation, or quiet contemplation.

The one member of the family who could not fully experience the beautifully landscaped grounds at Cottage Lawn was Julia, the eldest of three Higinbotham daughters. Confined to a wheelchair for most of her life, she spent much of her time in the family parlor. Therefore, it is ironic that an incident in Julia's life, recounted by her sister Lily, offers us the best description of the semicircular flower garden at Cottage Lawn, which was located directly below the parlor window.

In "Wisteria's Mission," an essay published in 1895, Lily tells of a tendril of wisteria which gradually found its way into the parlor through a crack in the bottom of the bay window. Upon discovering it, Julia's nurse cried out, ". . . here behind the blind is a little green vine nearly a foot long — it is coming right in under the window."[20] The story goes on to tell of the wisteria's growth in the parlor, the amusement it brought to Julia that summer, and the poetic inspiration it provided her the very first day it was discovered.

Through her story about the wisteria vine and the way it touched her sister's life, Lily also confirms that there were "tall trees on the lawn" and that a "trumpet creeper" (*Campsis radicans*) swayed in the wind on an arbor just outside the bay window. "In May . . . tulips looked up gaily from under the windows, and the lilac bushes held up their fleecy white bouquets to the sun . . ." The narrative also mentions that ". . . one bright day, the man came to carry the houseplants into the garden . . . [putting them] down upon the coveted earth . . . [among the] gay nasturtiums, and sweet peas."[21] This description is particularly valuable, since historical photographs of the garden yield little information about its organization and detail.

Although Cottage Lawn was created less than a decade after the publication of Downing's influential *Treatise on the Theory and Practice of Landscape Gardening* (1841), it appears to have contained all the characteristic elements of the modern or natural style of landscape gardening: a large lawn, groves of trees in natural-looking groups, gently curving paths and drives which afforded changing views of the Gothic cottage and grounds, and a fancy flower garden placed where it could be enjoyed from both inside and out. The very choice of this style attests to the education and taste of the Higinbotham family; but it was skill in combining landscape elements which created both a picturesque composition and a comfortable home. Cottage Lawn was a well designed country residence whose landscape met the functional needs of a family at mid-century, and whose "picturesque" ornamental grounds were in perfect harmony with the architecture of their English style cottage.

7.23 View of West Façade, "Cottage Lawn," Oneida, New York, October 1864
Collection of the Madison County Historical Society, Oneida, New York

This is the earliest documented photographic view of Cottage Lawn. Typical of Gothic Revival cottages are the carved vergeboards ornamenting the gables, the tracery window designs, and decorative chimneys. The rather roughly cut lawn with its ornamental plantings provides the foreground for the view. The flower garden can be seen at the extreme right near the residence. Note the rose obelisk painted white in the center of the garden.

7.24 "Cottage Lawn" from Grove Street, 1886
Collection of the Madison County Historical Society, Oneida, New York

This image documents several elements of the landscape garden at Cottage Lawn. Vines supported by ornamental trellises enframed the windows, while shrubs, most notably a smoketree (*Cotinus coggygria*) with its distinctive fluffy panicles, accented the corners of the veranda. Surrounding the property was a Gothic style fence which complemented the architecture of the residence. In the foreground were sugar maples (*Acer saccharum*) planted at regular intervals along the three streets which bordered the property.

7.25 Gothic Garden Pavilion at "Cottage Lawn," c. 1895
Collection of the Madison County Historical Society, Oneida, New York

This diminutive garden structure stood just south of the residence in a grove of tall evergreens. The trees in the distance may line the banks of Higinbotham Brook where it touched the southern property line of Cottage Lawn. This woodland setting, traversed by naturalistic paths and drives, must have been a favorite spot at Cottage Lawn, since it was the subject of several photographs. Pictured here are Miss Louise Higinbotham and Dr. A. V. Needham.

"Sonnenberg," Canandaigua, New York
A Half-Century of Garden-Making

The gardens of Sonnenberg were developed by Mr. and Mrs. Frederick Ferris Thompson over a period of nearly fifty years. Canandaigua was the girlhood home of Mrs. Thompson, the former Mary Lee Clark, and continued to be the Thompson's summer residence throughout their entire lives. Today, Sonnenberg Gardens and Mansion are operated by a nonprofit educational corporation, and the fifty acre estate is open to the public.

Mary Clark Thompson was the daughter of Myron Holley Clark, who was elected governor of New York State in 1854. It was during the family's residence in Albany that Mary met Frederick Ferris Thompson, a New York City banker and the publisher of a financial newsletter. After a brief courtship, they were married in Canandaigua in 1857.

For their permanent residence, the Thompsons maintained a Madison Avenue townhouse in New York, but summers were spent with the Clark family in Canandaigua. In 1863, they purchased Sonnenberg from the Holberton family and developed it as their summer home. Its name, translated literally, meant "sunny hill," a most appropriate description of the hilltop setting.

Sonnenberg soon gained a reputation for spacious lawns, beautiful flower gardens and the generous hospitality of its owners. In 1866, a young visitor revealed, "We went to a lawn fete at Mrs. F. F. Thompson's this afternoon. It was a beautiful sight. The flowers, the grounds, the young people and the music all combined to make the occasion perfect."[22] During the same period, Mr. Thompson, who was an amateur stereographer, took the first photographs of Sonnenberg. They reveal not only the appearance of the gardens and grounds, but the activities of family and friends—at archery, croquet, and even garden tasks.

During the third quarter of the nineteenth century, few properties in western New York could rival Sonnenberg for elaborateness and extent of grounds. The earliest plan, surveyed and drawn by S. D. Backus in 1879, shows that extensive gardens and grounds had already been created. The areas south and east of the residence featured large lawns, with specimen trees planted at the margins. The flower garden extended to the west, from the residence to the vicinity of the greenhouse. Large areas were also devoted to the cultivation of vegetables and fruit.

The flower garden was, perhaps, one of the most interesting features at Sonnenberg. Although its organization was traditional, the plantings were carried out in a unique fashion. The garden consisted of large panels of grass, roughly rectangular in shape, with cross paths of gravel. Within each grass panel were single flower beds arranged in different ways. Some panels were restricted to beds with geometric shapes—circles, ellipses, and commas—while others featured long, narrow borders. There were symmetrical beds which resembled parterres, as well as irregular beds with seemingly random arrangement.

Taken together, they represented many of the various bedding styles which were at the height of fashion.

As the gardens of Sonnenberg evolved, so too did the residence. In 1887, the Thompsons built a new house on top of the hill. The forty room mansion, designed by Boston architect Francis Allen, "fit into the landscape so quietly and naturally that it seems always to have been there." One of the most delightful characteristics about its design was the way interior and exterior interpenetrated. "As we draw near enough to take in some of the external details of the house, with its mantle of green ivy, and a dozen other vines, its awnings, its porches and its balconies, each feature has the word COMFORT written all over it."[23]

With the end of the nineteenth century, the first chapter of the gardens at Sonnenberg came to a close. Frederick Ferris Thompson died in 1899, leaving Mary Clark Thompson a sizable inheritance. They had no children, but in the words of her nephew, "She loved her hometown with the same loyal affection which she gave to her family."[24] Although she retained their Madison Avenue townhouse as her principal residence, she returned faithfully to Canandaigua to fulfill a mission of her own: the renovation of the gardens at Sonnenberg.

Mary Clark Thompson articulated the importance of her garden in a poem she composed in 1873, when she was thirty-eight years old. Perhaps, as she approached her sixty-fifth year, the words took on new meaning. The first two verses and the last two verses follow:

Within my garden fair and sweet,
My thoughts full often stray,
To greet again the lovely flowers
Along the accustomed way.

I see once more my treasures bright
Fresh springing, ever new,
Fair blossoms opening to the light,
And sparkling with the dew.

In those cool shades, those sunny paths,
My heart forgets her care,
Though weak my faith, though crushed my hopes,
They'll bud and blossom there.

Should sorrow darken all my path,
And cloud my future years,
The sunshine in my garden will
Make rainbows of my tears.[25]

The second chapter of the gardens at Sonnenberg began without delay. In 1900, Ernest N. Bowditch, a Boston landscape architect, prepared a master plan for Sonnenberg which proposed reorganizing the gardens and grounds. After numerous revisions, the new gardens began to take shape, beginning with the Italian Garden in 1902. Bold in conception, brilliant in execution, it was more reminiscent of the Baroque gardens of France than of Italian Renaissance gardens. Views from the library were extended out into the landscape: from the French doors, down the central walk, past the ancient Italian wellhead, to the Fountain of Hercules. "This is a garden to be traversed toward the four points of the compass, on its two axes and along all four of its boundaries. Like an orchestra opening with a flourish of all instruments, it swims into view from the house terrace like a symphony of formal floral designs, small conifers and box trees, marble vases, stone pillars and various other architectural features, all as harmonious as if a skilled artist had blocked out the entire color scheme from one setting of his palette, without a jarring note."[26]

With the success of the Italian Garden, more gardens followed, each with a different cultural or artistic theme. The Japanese Garden was created over a six-month period during 1906. With a crew of seven, the Japanese designer K. Wadamori transformed a smooth sloping lawn into a little valley, which dropped by pools and cascades through the garden. The centerpiece of this composition was an Oriental Tea House. "The first long-distance view of this Japanese Garden reveals a garden of exquisite touches. Every sweep of the eye embraces a gem-like lily pool or a brook; rocks that look as if they grew there, stone jewels of garden architecture, and statues that fit their surroundings. All these are set in exquisite rolling and sloping green turf garnished with conifers of at least nine shades of green."[27] Unlike the Italian Garden, where the whole idea could be grasped at once, the Japanese Garden revealed itself little by little.

During the first decades of the twentieth century, even more gardens and garden features were added. The Rose Garden, containing over five thousand rose bushes, extended like an amphitheater around a classical columned belvedere. Nearby, but hidden from view, was the Sub Rosa or Secret Garden, conceived in elegant simplicity with walls of green shrubbery and accents of marble figures. A nostalgic note was struck with the Old-Fashioned Garden, which featured boxwood edged beds filled with a tangle of flowers.

Many of Sonnenberg's gardens were created with the aid of John Handrahan, originally with the Bowditch firm, and subsequently employed by Mrs. Thompson exclusively. For her, Handrahan created the Pansy Garden, devoted to a favorite flower; and the Blue and White Garden, a garden room furnished only with flowers of blue and white. Admittedly her favorite, Mrs. Thompson preferred to call it her Intimate Garden. Handrahan was also responsible for the Moonlight Garden, one of the most unusual gardens at Sonnenberg. With white flowers whose fragrance and inflorescence could only be experienced after dark, ". . . the spell of the Moonlight Garden of Sonnenberg is not to be captured in the bright beams of gladsome day. Go at night, after moonrise, and give yourself to the romantic charm of the Place and the Hour."[28]

Handrahan's skill was not restricted to gardens of intimate proportions. It was he who meticulously engineered the five-acre Rock Garden, considered by one observer to be among the best in America. "Picture to yourself a wholly commonplace little hollow in a not-especially-interesting wood; with not a stone of its own in it, and no approach leading to it. Imagine no stone available for the needs of a rock garden anywhere nearer than thirty miles. Imagine a man of ordinary talents taking such a spot, and attempting to make out of it, or rather, in defiance of it, a Rock Garden fit for the gods that dwell on high Olympus!"[29] Handrahan was assisted in his efforts by Robert Ballantyne, who was responsible for the herbaceous planting. The overall effect of the ensemble was of total naturalness. "There are rocks a-many; but they do not . . . oppress you, as some rocks do. There are flowers in profusion; but they seem wild and self-sown. There is a broad median ribbon of green velvet turf; but it does not look handmade. The summer house invites you to rest a-while; but it fits into the spot and the design with a naturalness that is soothing and restful."[30]

The Rock Garden, built in 1916, was one of the last gardens constructed at Sonnenberg. In the years to follow, Mrs. Thompson shared her creation with the community she knew and loved. She opened her gardens and grounds frequently to the public, attracting as many as seven thousand people in a single day. She also entertained many distinguished guests and invited each to plant a tree. The gardens which began as a tribute to her husband, lived on in tribute to beauty and generous hospitality.

Following Mrs. Thompson's death in 1923, the estate passed to her nephew, Emory Wendell Clark. In 1931, he sold Sonnenberg to the United States Government for construction of the Veterans Administration Medical Center on the estate farmlands. Fortunately, the siting of the new facilities did not require the demolition of the mansion or dismantling of the gardens. For the next forty years, the Veterans Administration served as custodians of the estate. In 1972, President Nixon conveyed fifty acres to "Sonnenberg Gardens," a nonprofit educational corporation chartered to preserve, restore, and interpret the gardens and mansion to the public. In May of 1973, the gardens were opened to the public for the first time since Mrs. Thompson's famous "public days."

7.26 The Original Flower Garden Looking East toward the Residence, c. 1870
Collection of Sonnenberg Gardens, Canandaigua, New York

This panel of the flower garden featured only flower beds with regular geometric shapes: circles, ovals, commas or paisley shapes, and ellipses. Each was filled with annual plants to contrast dramatically with the smooth lawn. The dense hedge at left separated this garden from a more informal area to the north.

7.27 The Original Flower Garden Looking West from the Residence (opposite of
**   previous view), c. 1870**
Collection of Sonnenberg Gardens, Canandaigua, New York

The flower garden consisted of nearly a dozen panels of grass containing flower beds of various shapes. This view is the reverse of the previous one, showing the geometric shaped beds in the foreground. The panel beyond featured two long, narrow borders aligned parallel to the principal garden paths. The path at left was the central east-west axis to the garden.

**7.28 The Original Flower Garden Looking North toward the Greenhouse, c. 1870
Collection of Sonnenberg Gardens, Canandaigua, New York**

Although the main axis of the flower garden was oriented east-west, a cross-axis extended north in the vicinity of the greenhouse. This part of the garden featured small flower beds, a collection of ornamental shrubs and roses, and plants in pots set out from the greenhouse at the intersections of paths. Visible at right midground is a gardener with a mechanical lawn mower.

**7.29 View of the Mansion Looking North over the Ponds and Lawn, c. 1910
Collection of the Ontario County Historical Society, Canandaigua, New York**

This photograph shows the reorganization of the grounds at Sonnenberg initiated in 1900. Trees were planted in natural-looking groups on the lawns to create "windows" which revealed glimpses of the residence. The pond in the foreground was a natural feature, enhanced by skillful design and planting. The result was a park-like setting evocative of the romantic landscapes of England.

7.30 View of the Italian or Formal Garden from the Mansion, "Sonnenberg," 1913
Collection of the Ontario County Historical Society, Canandaigua, New York

Despite its name, the Italian Garden was not purely Italian in organization and detail. This elevated view from the mansion illustrates the symmetry which was characteristic of many European gardens during the seventeenth century. The fleur-de-lis pattern was repeated in each quadrant, requiring the installation each spring of 25,000 plants. These flower beds were set below the level of the surrounding paths so that strollers could appreciate the elaborate design from a better perspective. Also inspired by old European gardens was the topiary work: trees and shrubs clipped into artificial forms. These living sculptures had particular appeal before the plant explorations of the nineteenth century, when there was little variety among evergreens. They were used here to enhance the geometry of the design.

7.31 The Japanese Garden at "Sonnenberg," 1913
Collection of the Ontario County Historical Society, Canandaigua, New York

This photograph reveals all the essential elements of the Japanese Garden: water, rocks, evergreen plantings, Oriental architecture, and ornament. This naturalistic landscape of varied and intricate character was created from a broad sloping lawn southwest of the Italian Garden.

7.32 The Sub Rosa or Secret Garden, "Sonnenberg," c. 1910
Collection of the Ontario County Historical Society, Canandaigua, New York

The simplicity of this private garden in green and white contrasted sharply with the adjacent Rose Garden, which featured wave after wave of colorful blossoms. The allegorical figure which forms the centerpiece of the garden is Bacchante, flanked by the Four Seasons. Spring at left, carries a bouquet of irises; Summer, opposite, a shaft of wheat. Autumn and Winter (not visible) present grapes of the vine and oak leaves.

7.33 The Old Fashioned or Colonial Garden, "Sonnenberg," c. 1910
Collection of the Ontario County Historical Society, Canandaigua, New York

This pergola, which extends from north to south, bisects the Old-Fashioned or Colonial Garden. On either side are two rectangular quadrants, each divided into four triangular beds by paths which intersect on the diagonal. Each bed is surrounded by a low edging of boxwood and filled with a varied assortment of perennial plants. The peony beds in the foreground are separated from the formal garden by a low barberry hedge.

Other Photographs of Sonnenberg

NOTES

1—Gardens of the Gilded Age

1. Richardson Wright in Henry Stuart Ortloff, *A Garden Bluebook of Annuals and Biennials* (Garden City: Doubleday, Page & Company, 1924), p. x.

2. Walter E. Houghton, *The Victorian Frame of Mind: 1830–1870* (New Haven: Yale University Press, 1979), p. 1; also *The Gilded Age,* edited by H. Wayne Morgan, revised edition (Syracuse: Syracuse University Press, 1975), p. 2; and Arthur Meier Schlesinger, *The Rise of Modern America 1865–1951* (New York: Macmillan, 1959), p. 55. Change was not a characteristic applied to the nineteenth century only in retrospect: it was recognized as an active force by those who experienced the period. "There has never been in the history of civilization," observed Edward Atkinson in 1891, "a period, or a place, or a section of the earth in which science and invention have worked such progress or have created such opportunity for material welfare as in these United States in the period which has elapsed since the end of the civil war." Schlesinger, *The Rise of Modern America,* p. 29.

3. Houghton, *The Victorian Frame of Mind,* p. 6.

4. At no time was the relationship of society and nature, of city and country, more studied in America than in the nineteenth century. For a more detailed analysis of the impact of technology on intellectual and creative endeavors see Leo Marx, *The Machine in the Garden* (New York: Oxford University Press, 1964).

5. Nathaniel Hawthorne, *The American Notebooks,* edited by Randall Stewart (New Haven: Yale University Press, 1932), pp. 102–105.

6. Once upon a time, "people did not run about the town or the land as we do. They travelled less often, did not hurry to catch trains, wrote one letter a morning instead of ten. Now, we are whirled about, and hooted around and rung up as if we were all parcels, booking clerks or office boys." Houghton, *The Victorian Frame of Mind,* p. 7.

7. Schlesinger, *Rise of Modern America,* p. 45.

8. Ibid., pp. 40–45.

9. Ibid., p. 127.

10. Ibid.

11. Marx, *Machine in the Garden,* p. 228.

12. Henry David Thoreau explodes the rural myth with comments on the "nobility" of the farmer: "I respect not his labors, his farm where everything has its price, who would carry the landscape, who would carry his God, to market, if he could get anything for him; who goes to market for his god as it is." In Marx, *Machine in the Garden,* p. 258.

13. George Tatum, "The Emergence of an American School of Landscape Design: The Contributions of A. J. Downing and F. L. Olmsted." Paper presented at Lyndhurst, National Trust for Historic Preservation, June 20, 1970.

14. Andrew Jackson Downing, *Rural Essays,* edited by George William Curtis (New York: Leavitt and Allen, 1857), pp. 139–42.

15. Tatum, "Emergence of an American School of Landscape Design."

16. Charles Dudley Warner, *My Summer in A Garden* (Boston: James R. Osgood and Company, 1872), p. 15.

17. In 1846, Alexander Mack described the village of Canandaigua: "The main road between Buffalo and Albany which passes through it, constitutes its principal street . . . which is about a mile long, is exceedingly wide, and shaded on either side by an unbroken succession of lofty and magnificent trees. The houses on both sides, which are almost all detached from each other, are some distance back from the street, having gardens in front occupied by grass and flower plots, with clumps of green foliage overhead." In Roger Haydon, *Upstate Travels: British Views of Nineteenth-Century New York* (Syracuse: Syracuse University Press, 1982), p. 189.

18. Lewis Mumford, *The City in History* (New York: Harcourt, Brace & World, 1961), p. 489.

19. William Rose Benet, *The Reader's Encyclopedia* (New York: Thomas Y. Crowell, 1948), p. 943.

20. Irving's *Sketchbook* (1819) and Cooper's *Leatherstocking Tales* (1823–41) were best sellers in America as well as Europe.

21. Katherine Kuh, *Art in New York State. The River: Places and People.* (Buffalo: The Buffalo Fine Arts Academy, 1964).

22. Russell Lynes, *The Art-Makers* (New York: Dover Publications, 1982; originally published in 1970 by Atheneum, New York, as *The Art-Makers of Nineteenth Century America*), p. 214.

23. Lewis Mumford, *Roots of Contemporary American Architecture* (New York: Grove Press, 1952), p. 423.

24. In the second edition of Downing's *Treatise on the Theory and Practice of Landscape Gardening* (1844), he writes, "There is no part of the Union where the taste in landscape gardening is so far advanced as on the middle portion of the Hudson."

25. Norman T. Newton, *Design on the Land: The Development of Landscape Architecture* (Cambridge: Harvard University Press, 1974), p. 266. Downing inculcated many aristocratic ideals, among them that gardens were a measure of civilized society. In 1845, when most of New York State was still frontier, he wrote, "So long as men are forced to dwell in log huts and follow the hunter's life, we must not be surprised at lynch law and the use of the bowie knife. But when smiling lawns and tasteful cottages begin to embellish a country, we know that order and culture are established." In Russell Lynes, *The Tastemakers* (New York: Harper & Brothers, 1954), p. 21.

26. Hudson River properties of note included Hyde Park (laid out by André Parmentier), Blithewood at Barrytown, Montgomery Place, Ellerslie, Linwood, The Locusts near Rhinebeck, Netherwood and High Cliff near New Hamburg, and Wodenethe (laid out by H. W. Sargent).

27. Frederica Bremer, *The Homes of the New World* (New York: Harper, 1853), p. 46.

28. Calvert Vaux in Lynes, *The Tastemakers,* p. 32.

29. In 1850, Downing convinced a young English architect, Calvert Vaux, to join him in America as his partner. Seven years later, after Downing's death, Vaux invited Frederick Law Olmsted to collaborate on a plan for Central Park in Manhattan. The two entered their "Greensward" plan into the competition and won.

30. The social and political aims of Central Park are revealed in the official description of the "Greensward" plan by Vaux and Olmsted: "The primary purpose of the Park is to provide the best practical means of healthful recreation for the inhabitants of all classes. . . . It is the one great purpose of the Park to supply to the hundreds of thousands of tired workers, who have no opportunity to spend their summers in the country, a specimen of God's handiwork that shall be to them, inexpensively, what a month or two in the White Mountains or the Adirondacks is, at great cost, to those in easier circumstances." Second Annual Report, Central Park Commissioners, January 1, 1859, p. 44. Cited in Bruce Kelly, Gail Travis Guillet, and Mary Ellen W. Hern, *Art of the Olmsted Landscape,* (New York: The Arts Publisher, 1981), p. 79.

31. Central Park was not the first public park designed in the natural style in America. In 1853, a fifty acre park was created from the slums of Hartford, Connecticut. It was later named Bushnell Park, for the gentleman who first proposed it, fought for it, and was responsible for its romantic design. John Brinckerhoff Jackson, *American Space: The Centennial Years, 1865–1876* (New York: W. W. Norton, 1972), p. 215

32. Calvert Vaux, cited in Albert Fein, *Frederick Law Olmsted and the American Environmental Tradition* (New York: George Braziller, 1972), p. 13.

33. For a fuller discussion of Olmsted's public parks, see Bruce Kelly, Gail Travis Guillet, and Mary Ellen W. Hern, *Art of the Olmsted Landscape* (New York: The Arts Publisher, 1981).

34. Beauty in the landscape was a symbol not of an enlightened social order, as it had been a century before, but of a divine purpose for America. See John Brinckerhoff Jackson, "Several American Landscapes," *Landscapes: Selected Writings of J. B. Jackson,* edited by Ervin H. Zube (University of Massachusetts Press, 1970), p. 52.

35. "Stray Notes on Horticulture," *The Horticulturist* 4 (March 1850) p. 399.

36. David Maldwyn Ellis, "Rise of the Empire State, 1790–1820," in *New York History,* January 1975.

37. Paul W. Gates, "Agricultural Change in New York State, 1850–1890," in *New York History,* April 1969.

38. New York State nurserymen and seedsmen who established businesses prior to 1860 when this study begins include: James Bloodgood of Flushing (1798), Grant Thorburn of New York (1805), Charles Downing of Newburgh (c. 1810), Thomas Hogg of New York (1822), André Parmentier of Brooklyn (1825), Thomas Bridgeman of New York (c. 1830), Michael Floy of New York (c. 1830), Samuel B. Parsons of Flushing (1838), George Ellwanger and Patrick Barry of Rochester (1840) and Isaac Hicks of Westbury (1854). For more information on early American nurseries, see *Plants and Gardens* 23 (Brooklyn Botanic Garden, 1968).

39. Diane Holahan Grosso, "From the Genesee to the World" in *The Bulletin* 35 (University of Rochester Library, 1982), p. 4.

40. Lynes, *The Art-Makers,* p. 161.

41. "No part of the world is more richly blessed with soil and climate, for a great and flourishing agricultural interest than the western part of the state of New York—that part called OLD GENESEE." Luther Tucker in the *Genesee Farmer* (1831), cited in *The Garden of the Genesee* (Rochester: Rochester Historical Society, 1940), p. 11.

42. Ulysses Prentiss Hedrick, *A History of Horticulture in America to 1860* (New York: Oxford University Press, 1950), p. 242.

43. Ibid.

44. Ibid., p. 224.

45. Charles Van Ravenswaay, *A Nineteenth-Century Garden* (New York: The Main Street Press, 1977), p. 12.

46. William I. Aeberli and Margaret Becket, "Joseph Harris: Captain of the Rochester Seed Industry," *The Bulletin,* vol. 35 (University of Rochester Library, 1982), p. 74.

47. Anna Warner, who had been brought up in a comfortable middle-class home, was compelled to earn a living because of financial reverses. She exercised her talent for writing on the topic she knew best, amateur gardening. *Gardening By Myself* (New York: Anson D. F. Randolph, 1872) was directed to other women so they could turn to gardening for pleasure or profit, perhaps even achieving a degree of independence. Her advice was practical and her encouragement generous.

Peter Henderson was both a seedsman and a prolific author. In addition to the horticultural advice he put forth in his annual catalogs, he wrote *Gardening for Profit* (1868), *Practical Floriculture* (1869), *Gardening for Pleasure* (1875), *Henderson's Handbook of Plants* (1881), and *Garden and Farm Topics* (1884).

48. In 1870, Frank J. Scott wrote *The Art of Beautifying Suburban Home Grounds of Small Extent* and dedicated it "To the memory of A. J. Downing, his friend and instructor, . . . with affectionate remembrance." 1870 also marked the publication of *Beautifying Country Homes* by Jacob Weidenmann, an occasional collaborator of Frederick Law Olmsted. Both Scott and Weidenmann used scaled plans extensively throughout the texts. For greater insight on the state of landscape gardening at the close of the nineteenth century, see

Art Out-of-Doors by Mrs. Schuyler Van Rensselaer (New York: Charles Scribner's Sons, 1893 and 1911). Mrs. Van Rensselaer was also a frequent contributor to *Garden and Forest,* a fashionable gardening periodical which appeared between 1888 and 1897. A bibliography on "Gardening Art from 1625 to 1890" appears as the appendix of her book. The list was compiled by Henry Sargent Codman and first appeared in *Garden and Forest* 3 (March, 1890), p. 131.

49. Frank A. Waugh, *Landscape Gardening* (New York: Orange Judd Company, 1899), p. 5.

2—The Influence of Style and Dilemma of Taste

1. Frank A. Waugh, *Landscape Gardening,* second edition, revised (New York: Orange Judd, 1919), p. 15.

2. André Parmentier in "Landscapes and Picturesque Gardens" for Thomas Fessenden, *The New American Gardener* (Boston: J. B. Russell, 1828), p. 184–87.

3. Patrick Barry, "The Present and Future of American Horticulture," *The Horticulturist* 8 (January 1853), p. 12.

4. Downing elaborated on the distinction between the natural and formal styles in *The Horticulturist* 4 (August, 1849), pp. 57–60: "Among our countrymen at the present day, there are two distinct classes of taste in rural art; first, the poetic or northern taste, based on a deep instinctive feeling for nature; and second, the artistic or symmetric taste, based on a perception of the Beautiful, as embodied in works of art. The larger part of our countrymen . . . find most delight in the natural landscape garden; but [for others], the classic villa, with its artistic adornments of vase and statue, urn and terrace, is an object of much more positive pleasure than the most varied and seductive gardens laid out with the witchery of nature's own handiwork."

5. Neltje Blanchan, *The American Flower Garden* (New York: Doubleday, Page & Co., 1909), p. 121.

6. Fredericka Bremer, *The Homes of the New World* (New York: Harper, 1853), p. 46.

7. Calvert Vaux, *Villas and Cottages* (New York: Harper & Brothers, 1869).

8. William Cullen Bryant, "Thanatopsis," in F. O. Matthiessen, *The Oxford Book of American Verse* (New York: Oxford University Press, 1952).

9. Henry Winthrop Sargent, in Andrew Jackson Downing, *Treatise on the Theory and Practice of Landscape Gardening* (Sakonnet: Theophrastus Publishers, 1977 reprint of 9th Edition [1875]), p. 547.

10. Thomas Allen, "Notes on the State of Rural Arts," *The Horticulturist* 1 (September, 1846), p. 111.

11. Andrew Jackson Downing, *Cottage Residences,* 3rd edition (New York and London: Wiley and Putnam, 1847), p. 92.

12. Ibid., p. 144.

13. Andrew Jackson Downing, *Treatise on the Theory and Practice of Landscape Gardening,* 8th edition (New York: Orange Judd, 1858), p. 369.

14. Newspaper article, *The Radii* (Canajoharie, N. Y.), April 16, 1891.

15. Newspaper article, *Canajoharie Courier,* February 28, 1911.

16. Newspaper article, *The Radii* (Canajoharie, N. Y.), March 2, 1911.

17. Susan D. Plank, "The Arkells and their Gardens," unpublished paper, May 1982, Canajoharie Library and Art Gallery, Canajoharie, N. Y.

18. Newspaper article, *The Radii* (Canajoharie, N. Y.), August 19, 1880.

19. Frank J. Scott, *Victorian Gardens* (Watkins Glen: American Life Foundation, reprint of 1870, *The Art of Beautifying Suburban Home Grounds of Small Extent*), p. 22.

20. Andrew Jackson Downing, *Victorian Cottage Residences* (New York: Dover Publications, Inc.), reprint of 1873, *Cottage Residences,* p. 242.

21. Ibid.

22. Herbert Croly, "The Lay-out of a Large Estate," *Architectural Record* 16 (December, 1904), p. 555.

3—Verdant Frames: Landscape Elements and their Artful Arrangement

1. One garden critic, commenting on excessiveness in planting, observed that, "The more a man loves, in an unreasoning way, the works of nature, the more likely he is to think that he cannot have too many of them in his grounds, and no error is so fatal as this to a good general result. And the stronger his horticultural passion, the more apt he is to care about novelties and eccentricities—about conspicuous plants as such; and the profuse use of these gives the last fatal touch to the inartistic disorder of the usual overcrowded domain." Mrs. Schuyler Van Rensselaer, *Art Out-of-Doors* (New York: Charles Scribner's Sons, 1893), p. 49.

2. "On the Drapery of Cottages and Gardens," *The Horticulturist* 3 (February, 1849), p. 354.

3. Frank J. Scott *The Art of Beautifying Suburban Home Grounds of Small Extent* (New York: D. Appleton & Co., 1870), p. 105.

4. Roger Hale Newton, *Town and Davis, Architects* (New York: Columbia University Press, 1942), p. 268.

5. Andrew Jackson Downing, *Treatise on the Theory and Practice of Landscape Gardening,* 9th edition, with supplements (New York: Orange Judd, 1875), p. 19.

6. Ibid., p. 35.

7. "On the Drapery of Cottages and Gardens," p. 355.

8. D. W. Lothrop, "Changes in Rural Taste," *The Gardener's Monthly* 29 (May, 1887), p. 134.

4—Art Out-of-Doors: The Embellishment of the Grounds

1. Frank A. Waugh, *Landscape Gardening* (New York: Orange Judd, 1899), p. 24.

2. Rusticus [pseud.], "Design for a Rustic Gate," *The Horticulturist* 1 (August, 1846), p. 73.

3. Neltje Blanchan, *The American Flower Garden* (New York: Doubleday, Page & Co., 1909), p. 340.

4. James Vick, *Vick's Illustrated Catalog and Floral Guide,* (Rochester: James Vick, 1872), p. 119.

5. A. D. G., "Hints to Beginners in Ornamental Planting," *The Horticulturist* 10 (December, 1855), p. 545.

6. "Seasonable Hints—Flower Garden and Pleasure Ground," *The Gardener's Monthly* 29 (March, 1887), p. 65.

7. Blanchan, *The American Flower Garden,* p. 344.

8. Waugh, *Landscape Gardening,* p. 25.

9. Andrew Jackson Downing, *Cottage Residences,* 3rd edition (New York and London: Wiley and Putnam, 1847), p. 14.

10. Billie Sherrill Britz, *The Greenhouse at Lyndhurst: Construction and Development of the Gould Greenhouse, 1881* (Washington, D.C.: The Preservation Press, 1977), p. 20.

11. "Jay Gould's Conservatories at Irvington on the Hudson, N. Y.," *The Gardener's Monthly* 27 (August, 1885), p. 253.

12. In Lord and Burnham's greenhouse catalog of 1907, Mr. Burnham reminisced about early developments in the greenhouse industry. "Yes, enthusiasm has kept us always on the alert for new and better ways of doing things; has helped to make us pioneers along the line of structural improvements. For instance, they formerly used bulky wooden rafters which excluded much of the sunlight. We were the first to use steel rafters in place of wood. That was in 1881, on the big range of greenhouses built for the late Jay Gould. We were also the first to substitute cast iron sills and gutters in place of wood." Cited in Britz, *The Greenhouse at Lyndhurst,* p. 21.

13. Ibid., p. 24.

14. Blanchan, *The American Flower Garden,* p. 341.

15. Ibid., p. 28.

5—Flower Gardens: Great Effects by Small Means

1. Cited in Roger Haydon, *Upstate Travels: British Views of Nineteenth-Century New York* (Syracuse: Syracuse University Press, 1982), p. 189.

2. J. J. Thomas, "Grouping Flowers—A Suggestion," *The Horticulturist* 1 (September, 1846), p. 121.

3. Jacob Weidenmann, *Beautifying Country Homes,* (1870), reprinted as *Victorian Landscape Gardening* (Watkins Glen: American Life Foundation, 1978), p. 28.

4. Henry W. Cleaveland, William Backus, and Samuel D. Backus, *Village and Farm Cottages: The Requirements of American Village Homes* (1856), reprinted (Watkins Glen: American Life Foundation, 1976), p. 153.

5. Mrs. Schuyler Van Rensselaer, *Art Out-of-Doors* (New York: Charles Scribner's Sons, 1893), p. 308.

6. Neltje Blanchan, *The American Flower Garden* (New York: Doubleday, Page and Co., 1909), p. 70.

7. Ellwanger and Barry, *Mount Hope Nurseries General Catalog* (Rochester, N.Y., undated), p. 68.

8. J. Wilkinson Elliott, *A Plea for Hardy Plants* (New York: Doubleday, Page and Co., 1902), p. 14.

9. Blanchan, *The American Flower Garden,* p. 100.

10. Charles Henderson, *Henderson's Picturesque Gardens* (New York: Peter Henderson & Co., 1908), p. 117.

11. Peter Henderson, *Gardening for Pleasure* (New York: Orange Judd, 1885), p. 35.

12. John J. Thomas, *Illustrated Annual Register of Rural Affairs, for 1876–78* vol. 8 (Albany, N.Y.: Luther Tucker & Son, 1898), p. 133.

13. Anna Warner, *Gardening By Myself* (New York: Anson D. G. Randolph & Co., 1872), p. 62.

14. W. H. Taplin, "Plants for Bedding," *Garden and Forest* 2 (May, 1889), p. 246.

15. Van Rensselaer, *Art Out-of-Doors,* p. 160.

16. Blanchan, *The American Flower Garden,* p. 298.

17. Bernard M'Mahon, *The American Gardener's Calendar* (Philadelphia: B. Graves, 1806), p. 71.

18. Charles Henderson, *Henderson's Picturesque Gardens,* p. 90.

6—Maintaining the Image

1. John E. Sedding in Neltje Blanchan, *The American Flower Garden* (New York: Doubleday, Page and Co., 1909), p. 68.

2. Peter Henderson, *Practical Floriculture* (New York: Orange Judd, 1869), p. 14.

3. Anna Warner, *Gardening By Myself* (New York: Anson D. F. Randolph & Co., 1872), p. 62.

4. Edward Hazen, *The Panorama of Professions and Trades: or Every Man's Book* (Philadelphia: Euriah Hunt, 1837), reprinted as *Yesterday's Encyclopedia of Early American Trades* (Watkins Glen: Century House, 1970), p. 23.

5. Charles Dudley Warner, *My Summer in a Garden* (Boston: James R. Osgood and Co., 1872), p. 38.

6. An Old Digger [pseud.], "Practical Hints to Amateurs," *The Horticulturist* 4 (July, 1849), p. 19.

7. Dr. Fothergill, "Pleasures of Planting," *The Horticulturist* 10 (August, 1855), p. 381.

8. Thomas Fessenden, *The New American Gardener* (Boston: J. B. Russell, 1828), pp. 184–86.

9. James Vick, *Vick's Illustrated Catalogue and Floral Guide* (Rochester: James Vick, 1872), p. 5.

10. Peter Henderson, *Gardening for Pleasure* (New York: Orange Judd, 1885), p. 175.

11. Vick, *Vick's Illustrated Catalogue,* p. 119.

12. Bellamy Partridge and Otto Bettmann, *As We Were: Family Life in America, 1850–1900.* (New York and London: McGraw-Hill Book Co., 1946), p. 150.

13. Vick, *Vick's Illustrated Catalogue,* p. 121.

14. J. C. Furnas, *The Americans: A Social History of the United States, 1587–1914* (New York: G. P. Putnam's Sons, 1969), p. 813.

15. Arthur Meier Schlesinger, *The Rise of Modern America, 1865–1951* (New York: Macmillan, 1959), p. 143.

16. Andrew Jackson Downing, *Treatise on the Theory and Practice of Landscape Gardening,* 9th edition (New York: Orange Judd, 1875), reprinted (Sakonnet: Theophrastus Publishers, 1977), p. 20.

17. William Chorlton, "The Qualifications of a Good Gardener," *The Horticulturist* 8 (April, 1853), p. 178.

18. Ibid.

7—Photographic Portraits of Five New York State Gardens

1. Andrew Jackson Downing, *Treatise on the Theory and Practice of Landscape Gardening,* 9th edition (New York: Orange Judd, 1875), reprinted (Sakonnet: Theophrastus Publishers, 1977), p. 243.

2. Ibid., p. 343.

3. *Syracuse City Directory, 1870–71,* p. 29.

4. Ibid.

5. Newspaper article, *The Cazenovia Republican.* No date.

6. L. H. Bailey, "An Old-Time Home Garden," *Country Life in America* 3 (November, 1902), p. 20–21.

7. Helen Lincklaen Fairchild, *Lorenzo House-Book,* Lorenzo State Historic Site, Cazenovia, N. Y.

8. "Pine" was sometimes imprecisely applied to all evergreen trees. The specimens referred to were actually Norway spruces (*Picea abies*).

9. Fairchild, *Lorenzo House-Book.*

10. Ibid.

11. L. H. Bailey, "An Old-Time Home Garden."

12. Ibid.

13. Ruth Dean, *The Livable House, Its Garden* (New York: Moffat Yard and Co., 1917), p. 84.

14. Bessie Smith White, "Memories," May 1926, p. 6. Diary at Smithtown Historical Society, Smithtown, N. Y.

15. John A. Gade, "Mr. Stanford White's Home at St. James," *House and Garden* 3 (February, 1903), p. 201.

16. Ibid., p. 205.

17. Ibid., p. 206.

18. Andrew Jackson Downing, *Cottage Residences,* 3rd edition (New York and London: Wiley and Putnam, 1847), p. 24.

19. Ibid., p. vi.

20. L. R. H. and J. R. H., *Wisteria's Mission.* (New York: James Pott & Co., 1895), p. 16.

21. Ibid., p. 9–10.

22. Caroline Cowles Richards, *Village Life in America, 1852–1872.* (New York: Henry Holt and Co., 1913), p. 205.

23. William T. Hornaday, "Masterpieces in Garden-Making, or the Ten Creations of Mrs. Frederick Ferris Thompson" (unpublished manuscript, 1917, collection of Sonnenberg Gardens), p. 2.

24. Clark Williams in Lynda McCurdy Hotra, *Mary Clark Thompson, Canandaigua's Magnificent Benefactress* (Canandaigua, N.Y.: Ontario County Historical Society, 1984), p. 15.

25. Mary Clark Thompson in Hotra, p. 10.

26. Hornaday, "Masterpieces in Garden-Making," p. 14.

27. Ibid., p. 74.

28. Ibid., p. 95.

29. Ibid., p. 48.

30. Ibid., p. 52.

INDEX

Water-lily (*Nymphaea*), 26, 80, 87, 98, 102
Water systems, municipal, 102, 112
Waugh, Frank A., 11, 42, 74
Weidenmann, Jacob, 9, 42, 193
Westbury, New York, 193
White, Bessie Smith (Mrs. Stanford), 160; Lawrence Grant, 160; Stanford, 132, 160–69
Wickwire residence, Chester F., 34, 46, 100, 124
Williams residence (Utica, New York), 38
Williams residence, William P. (Manhattan, New York), 59, 82
Window boxes, 20, 74. *See also* Planters
Wisteria, 46, 171; Chinese (*W. sinensis*), 50
"Wisteria's Mission," 171–72
"Wodenethe," 192
Woman's Hardy Garden, A. (Ely), 150
Writers, garden, on cast-iron, 72; on Central Park, 6, 192; on design and planning, 12, 18, 28, 88, 195; on fences, 74; on flower beds, 52, 54, 85, 92, 104; on garden architecture, 58, 66; on gardeners, 111, 128; on gardening, 7, 10, 111, 114, 116, 118, 122; on garden ornament, 59, 70; on gardens, 11, 82, 96, 106, 108, 151; on the Gilded Age, 1; on the Hudson River valley, 192; on

Writers (*cont.*)
landscape gardening, 20, 44, 111, 128, 192, 194; on lawnmowers, 118; on natural scenery, 11, 16; on the natural style, 11; on rustic work, 68, 80; on vines, 35. *See also* Patrick Barry; Neltje Blanchan; A. J. Downing; Alice Morse Earle; Helena Rutherford Ely; Thomas Fessenden; Gertrude Jekyll; Jens Jensen; John Claudius Loudon; Bernard M'Mahon; Maurice Maeterlinck; Frank J. Scott; Mrs. Schuyler Van Rensselaer; Anna Warner; Charles Dudley Warner; Frank Waugh; Jacob Weidenmann
Writers, of American literature, 4, 50. *See also* William Cullen Bryant; James Fenimore Cooper; Ralph Waldo Emerson; Nathaniel Hawthorne; Washington Irving; Henry David Thoreau
Wrought iron, 72

Yates, Alonzo Chester, 135, 140
Yates Castle. *See* Renwick-Yates Castle
Yonkers, New York, 20, 34, 48, 50
Yucca filimentosa (Adam's Needle), 92

GARDENS OF THE GILDED AGE

was composed in 10-point Digital Compugraphic Garamond and leaded 2 points
by Metricomp;
with initial capitals in Arboret and special title page ornaments provided
by Job Litho Services,
and display type set in Renaissant
by Rochester Mono/Headliners;
printed sheet-fed offset on 60-pound, acid-free Warren's Old Style Wove,
Smyth sewn and bound over 88-point binders' boards in Joanna Arrestox B
by Maple-Vail Book Manufacturing Group, Inc.;
with dust jackets printed in two colors
by Philips Offset Co., Inc.;
designed by Will Underwood;
and published by

SYRACUSE UNIVERSITY PRESS
SYRACUSE, NEW YORK 13244-5160